Liberian Democracy

Liberian Democracy

A Critique of the Principle of Checks and Balances

Thomas Kaydor, Jr.

authorHOUSE®

AuthorHouse™
1663 Liberty Drive
Bloomington, IN 47403
www.authorhouse.com
Phone: 833-262-8899

Published by AuthorHouse   12/16/2020

ISBN: 978-1-4969-0446-1 (sc)
ISBN: 978-1-4969-0447-8 (e)

Contents

Dedication

I dedicate this book to my deceased father, Hon Thomas Saidy Bah Kaydor, Sr.; the people of Liberia; the victims of bad governance arising from the lack of checks and balances amongst the three branches of the Liberian Government; the people of Africa who struggle for the end of poverty, hunger and disease; the World at large, which cries for global peace and development; and to all comrades in the struggle for good governance, democracy, development, social and economic justice, equality and fair play.

Acknowledgements

I thank God for my parents, Thomas Saidy Bah Kaydor, Sr. and Louise Malie Yassah Carter-Kaydor. They sponsored my education. I acknowledge and appreciate the support and patience of my children (Helen Koumassa Dwehdy Kaydor, Jordan Dweh Kaydor, Thomaslen Nunnoh Kaydor, Raymond Kwiah Kaydor, Julius Sundayboy Kaydor and Alfred Carter Kaydor), and their mother, my dearest wife, Helen Gbarvo Yassah Garbo-Kaydor. I also wish to acknowledge the support of my brothers and sisters and all other family members, and Rev Bartholomew Bioh Colley for their commitment to ensuring that I achieve higher education for a prosperous life.

Thanks to the Joseph Jenkins Roberts Scholarship Foundation for its fully funded scholarship to me during my post graduate studies in International Relations at the Ibrahim Badamasi Babangida Graduate School of International Studies, University of Liberia. This book is a function of my graduate thesis, which further advanced my undergraduate thesis.

Least I forget, I would like to thank Dr Kettehkumeuhn E. Murray and Dr Sahr Abdullai Vandi for facilitating the JJ Roberts Scholarship award, and to Mr Zehyu Buehyu Wuduorgar, Mr Jackson Wonde, Jr, Mr Leonid Walter Dunn, and Mr William K. Kerkula for their continuous encouragement and support in reinforcing my dream to become an author. Congratulations to anyone who may have contributed to my education leading to the production of this book, but inadvertently not mentioned herein.

About the Author

Born 19 March 1973 in Harrisburg, Montserrado County, Thomas Kaydor, Jr. (Tom Kaydor) is presently a postgraduate student at the Crawford School of Economics and Governance/ Public Policy, Australian National University in Canberra, Australia where he is reading a dual post graduate degree (Master of Public Policy with emphasis in Development Policy, and Master of Diplomacy). He previously earned a M.A (Suma Cum Laude) in International Relations from the IBB Graduate School of International Studies, University of Liberia, B.A (Magna Cum Laude) in Political Science with emphasis in Comparative Government and Politics with History as Minor, University of Liberia. He graduated from the St. Francis High School in Pleebo, Maryland County.

Tom Kaydor holds several professional certificates and diplomas including a Diploma in International Programme on Management and Development of NGOs, Galilee International

Management Institute, Formerly Galilee College, Israel; Certificate-Human Rights Based Approach & Results Based Management in Development Programming, UN System Staff College, Turin, Italy, and a Postgraduate Diploma in Diplomacy and Negotiation from the Islamabad Foreign Service Academy, Pakistan. He also holds Certificates in Basic Psychosocial Skills (TOT), and Training for Transformation, (TOT)-Mother Pattern College of Health Sciences; ABC E-Certificate-Professional Writing Skills for Business and Administration, Alan Borman Communications, UK; Training in UN General Service Staff/Headquarters Salary Survey and UN Human Resource Management, Congo Brazzaville; Atlas (UNDP Financial Management Studies), Prince II Written and Online Examinations, Programme Management; Advanced and Basic Security in the Field; Gender Journey, Thinking Outside the Box; UN Prevention of Harassment & Sexual Harassment & Abuse of Authority in Work Place; Peace Building & Programme Management (TOT), RECEIVE Inc., and Computer Operation and Networking, CHEALE Vocational Institute, Liberia.

He also received several awards including, but not limited to Pilgrim Certificate: Jerusalem Pilgrim-fulfilled the Biblical calling and ascended to Jerusalem, the Holy City, Capital of Israel; Certificate: Yardenit Baptismal Site on the Jordan River; Certificate of Highest Honor, University of Liberia; Certificate of Achievement: Mathematics, St. Francis High School; Certificate of Social and Political Change in Liberia, New DEAL Movement. He maintains memberships in professional organizations, including United Nations Coordination Network, Member, UN Peace Building Cooperation Net; Member, Online UN Volunteer network; Member, Humanitarian Law Practice Network. He also served as Member (Staff Representative) UNDP Liberia Disciplinary Committee.

Tom Kaydor served as Assistant Minister for Afro Asian Affairs at the Ministry of Foreign Affairs where he oversaw and coordinated Liberia's diplomatic relations with Africa, Asia, the Middle East and the Pacific. Prior to this post he served as UN Coordination and Common Services Adviser at the UN System in Ethiopia. In this capacity, he provided the relevant advice on Common Services and harmonized business practices considering the UN reform-Delivering as One (DaO)- to the Operations Management Team (OMT), its Chair, and the UN Country Team. He supported increased inter-agency operational collaboration and efficiency. In particular, he supported improvement and expansion of Common Services through effective coordination with OMT; facilitation of knowledge sharing; ensuring strategic direction of CS, and assessment, management and implementation of Common Services.

Additionally, he respectively served as the first National Coordination Officer and UN Coordination Analyst (International Civil Servant)-Integrated Office of the DSRSG/RC/HC/RR-Liberia ensuring effective Country Office Support to the UN System/UN Country Team (UNCT), OMT and IAPT thereby increasing trust and confidence in Resident Coordinator System; cutting transaction costs and promoting UN reform through Joint Programme formulation and Implementation, supporting Delivering as One (DaO) initiative in Liberia; promoting assessment, planning and implementation of Common Services and Harmonized Business Practices. He previously served as Chief of Office Staff-Office of the Chairman on Executive, House of Representatives, Republic of Liberia; Field Supervisor RECEIVE/USAID/LCIP Social Reintegration Programme, Liberia; Psychosocial Officer, World Vision International ; Editor-in-Chief- Observation newspaper, Liberia; Registrar, Trinity Lutheran High School-then Matadi Lutheran School; and Teaching/Research Assistant at the University of Liberia, AMEU and AMEZU Universities in Liberia. He is married to Mrs Helen Yassah Garbo-Kaydor with six children and several dependents.

His extra-curricular Activities include, but not limited to, Standard Bearer, Independent Camp, University of Liberia Students Union elections (2001/02); Chairman, Student Unification

Thomas Kaydor, Jr.

Party (SUP), University of Liberia (2001/2002); Chairman, Membership, Recruitment and Mobilization committee, SUP, (2000/2001); Reporter, Varsity Pilot newspaper. He is one of the Incorporators, Liberia Foundation for Education (LIFE, Inc.); and Founder, Thomas Kaydor Scholarship Fund (2008-present). On Religious Leadership: Vice President, Men Department, Trinity Lutheran Parish (2007-Present); Board Member, Trinity Lutheran School (2005-2008); President, Monrovia District Lutheran Youth Fellowship (presided over 11 parishes in seven counties-1999/2001), Secretary, Trinity Lutheran Youth Fellowship (1997/1998); Secretary, Grand Lutheran Youth Fellowship; and Treasurer, Newaken Lutheran Youth Fellowship.

He extensively travels around Africa, Asia, Europe and the Americas. He has Key and professional skills in facilitation, training; Communication; Speech writing; editing; oratory; reading and comprehension skills. He served as a consultant to develop training module on Democratic governance in Liberia; Liberia Institute for Public Administration (2007); Facilitator, UNDP Annual Retreats (2008 & 2009); Facilitator, Common Services Retreat, Operations Management Team, United Nations Liberia (2008); Co-Facilitator, Common Services Training, United Nations Liberia (2008, and Facilitator, Operations Management Team Retreat, United Nations Liberia (2010).

Thomas Kaydor's work and study focus on Development, Governance and Public Policy.

Abstract

In a republican form of government, power rests with the people who elect their leaders to represent their interests and remove same (leaders) if the people's happiness and safety so require (Liberia Constitution 1985). Even though Liberia is a republic, the Legislature is dormant, thereby shifting domineering power to the Executive, headed by the President.

Historically, the Republic of Liberia did not experience intense presidential dominance from the date of the country's independence until the ascendancy of William V.S. Tubman to the presidency in 1943. Tubman established himself as the "father" of the state and head of all its institutions. This was possible because he was the first president to have brought in and signed several mining concessional agreements with foreign businesses and investors. Tubman accrued enormous wealth from those concessions thus making him the most influential statesman in the country then. The then international and economic system, nepotism and one-party system gave him too much power to rule autocratically. Succeeding presidents to Tubman continued the autocracy of the presidency owing to weak, many a time, inept, inexperienced and impoverished legislators.

Although the presidential cult in Liberia germinated during the Tubman era, legislators themselves are predominantly responsible for the domineering presidency in the state. Many a time, majority of Liberia's legislators are either illiterate or semi-literate, and or ill informed about public policy making. They more often than not lack thorough understanding of their duties and responsibilities, least to talk about the intricacies occasioning the issue of checks and balances in a republican form of governance, the operation of national government, understanding of the international socioeconomic, political and diplomatic dynamics and legislative techniques. Sometimes the few literate or "educated" ones come to the legislature as inexperienced and impoverished individuals, thereby making them gullible to financial gains leading to the dollarization of legislative processes through receipt of bribes and huge lobby fees. These bribes and extravagant lobby fees dictate the enactment of laws against the national interest of the state and the general population.

The executive collects revenues, stores and expends them. Hence, gullible and indigent legislators become subservient to the Head of State who proffers money to woo legislative support in times of making critical political decisions, some of which are against the national interest of the state and its people.

The legislators sometimes neglect the use of their constitutional power to approve the scrupulous use of the country's resources during national budget formulation processes. They place emphasis on their amenities and benefits in the national budget as opposed to allocating substantive resources to pertinent national development priorities thereby negatively affecting the state and its people. The Chief Executive, in many instances, uses money and other emoluments to convince them pursue presidential agenda rather than an all-inclusive agenda agreed by all branches of the government and the people.

Another factor responsible for presidential dominance is the people's failure to elect competent and well knowledgeable persons to the legislature. Similarly, the public fails in holding legislators accountable. Generally, the elections of lawmakers in Liberia have been influenced by persons, parties, emotions and sometimes tribalism, instead of issues based on public policies and national interest.

Furthermore, majority of the citizens do not have access to the correct civic and voter education that would allow them vote for the rightful candidates. This can be blamed on the civil society and the national government. First, the civil society sometimes lacks the will power and resources to adequately educate the citizens on electoral matters. Some civil society agents advocate and gain public recognition that would later lead them to top political positions in which they entrench the very elitism they advocated against. Second, the government deliberately downplays civic and voter education fearing that this would empower citizens to gain insights in the operations, rights and obligations, duties and responsibilities of government, thereby providing critique of the political system. As a result of the foregoing, constituents blindly elect representatives and senators based either on kinship, campaign finances, fraternity, political parties, and or just on mere popularity, thereby begging the question of who is really fit to serve in such capacity.

A combination of the aforementioned factors results into the formulation of policies that victimize, marginalize and neglect the rights holders (citizens or electorates). Legislators enact laws that serve the interest of the elites rather than the mass population of the citizens.

However, this trend of a powerful presidency can be reversed if legislators become independent in their thought, actions, deeds, and when they are well abreast of their constitutional duties and responsibilities and check the other two branches of government in the true spirit and intent of the Liberian Constitution. Equally, lawmakers need the requisite knowledge and experience to be effective and efficient. They need to have the knowhow to formulating pro-poor policies entrenched by and anchored on Human Rights Principles and Results Based Management.

Thomas Kaydor, Jr.

If the government and civil society, as duty bearers, empower the electorates, they may likely elect the appropriate legislators who will enact laws for the common good of the people, be forthright with their duties, and exhibit the independence of the "first branch of government". The constituents themselves need to rise to the call to demand that their representatives do the right things or remove those (legislators) through the ballot box, if they fail to so do.

CHAPTER I

THE CONCEPTUAL PARADIGM

1.1. Background:

The Republic of Liberia has three branches of government that ought to be equal and coordinate based on the principle of checks and balances as enshrined in Article III of the Constitution. From 1848 to 1943 the legislature was "independent" (Sawyer 1992). They were "independent" because they originated predominantly from the settler minority whose regime was united based on common historical ties, fraternity and common identity in general. Simply put, members of the settlers' community shared common values and beliefs. More besides, they had basic education and insight for the management of a state. For instance, the first elected legislators, during the adoption and or approval of the constitution of the First Republic on September 27, 1847, had basic education as majority of them became drafters of the Declaration of Independence and the Constitution (Guannu 2000).

Also, legislators were merchants, business tycoons or former government officials. As such they had appreciable financial and economic independence. For example, before becoming president, Mr. Edward J. Roye, like many other politicians in the First Republic, was a wealthy and educated merchant. He effectively served as a Representative and Speaker as well as a Chief Justice (The Newark Advocate 1984). The legacy he left in these positions must have paved his way as the first darker complexioned Liberian to ascend to the presidency. However, this does not necessarily presuppose that prior experience in government must be the basis of becoming a legislator. Sometimes recycled politicians use looted resources to attain and further expand power. This should be discouraged in Liberia's democratic process. The point here is that lawmakers need to be people who are imbued with the strong believe that their work is a service to the people and country, rather than an opportunity to amass wealth at the detriment of the state and its people.

In the past, the legislature exhibited its power either by ensuring that the executive conformed to what it legislated. In some cases, it removed presidents and other government officials who violated the laws of the land. A classic case in point is the impeachment of Vice President James Smith by the House of Representatives after the deposition of President E. J. Roye in 1871 (Guannu 2000; The Newark Advocate 1984). It is my view that James Smith was removed to prevent another dark-skin presidency like E.J Roye's, and I think he should be recorded in Liberian history as a former President because of the three-month period he served as Acting President just like Former President Moses Blah who served for three weeks to end the term of Mr. Charles Taylor, after his resignation in August 2003 due to international pressure. Notably, President Roye had a controversy with the legislature over the extension of the tenure of a president from two years to four. This controversy, coupled with the issue of the 1871 loan, largely contributed to President Roye's forceful removal from office in 1871.

Another display of the strength of the Legislature was in 1900 when both the House of Representatives and the Liberian Senate, with the cabinet of President William D. Coleman, withdrew their support from the interior policies of the president, thus leading to his immediate resignation in an apparent fear of impeachment (Guannu 2000). The predominantly settler legislature remained somewhat independent up to 1944 when

President William V.S. Tubman ascended to power. Under Tubman, the legislature's independence diminished. One reason for this was that Tubman allowed more indigenous illiterate representatives in the first branch of government where he used them as pawns to accomplish his political motives. Even though it was good to have the indigenes represented in the government, their representation was intended to keep Tubman in power. He handpicked illiterate chiefs and elders that were subservient to him. These legislators were not popularly elected by their constituents. Even if they were elected, they lacked the capacity to make laws in the interest of their people. In May 1946, Tubman's constitutional amendment seeking the representation of the Provinces in parliament was granted. This allowed him the opportunity to pack the Legislature with his stooges as representatives.

Additionally, Tubman enunciated an "Open Door Policy" that allowed massive foreign direct investment, foreign concessions and businesses in the country. The Legislature ratified the concessional agreements, but the president exclusively received huge grafts, gifts, financial and material gains that made him wealthier than the state. With the enormous finances, the presidency was bound to use financial and economic influence in cajoling the other two branches of government into submission. In many instances when legislators strangely became radical and unwilling to succumb to the president, they were expelled, asked to resign or appointed to judicial or cabinet positions, thereby quieting their radicalism.

Fundamentally, there were three factors that led to presidential autocracy in the First Republic during Tubman's regime. First, President Tubman was a protector of Americo-Liberian interests; but equally, in 1946, he gave the indigenous majority the power to vote, and as well granted women suffrage. Second, the President was head and boss of the singular ruling party, which led the one-party state; and last, he was a dispenser of goods, services, and economic benefits. Besides these fundamental factors, Mr. Tubman used presidential and fraternal powers to manipulate the Legislature and Judiciary.

The legislators themselves have got serious moral and integrity problems. For instance, some legislators beg Caucasian traders las well as their Middle Eastern and Asian counterparts like Lebanese and Indians for goods and financial emoluments. Worse more, majority of the electorates are illiterate, and so are the legislators themselves. The mass illiteracy on the one hand disallows the citizens from critically and rationally analyzing those wanting to represent them. Equally, the illiterate or semi-literate lawmakers lack the ability to adequately and judiciously carry out their duties and responsibilities. It seems that illiteracy was a weapon of control over the majority indigenous population to allow the settlers have a free ride in running the affairs of the state. Today, illiteracy is still entrenched in the Liberian society.

Although there is greater opportunity for the indigenous to get higher education, nowadays, many of the lawmakers enter the legislature before enrolling at academic institutions. The former and current Speakers, as well as several other law makers of House of Representatives of the 52nd and 53rd Legislature, the former President Pro-Tempore of the Senate the 52nd Legislature, use their legislative powers and positions to enroll at universities, thus undermining credible admission procedures at various institutions of learning. Today, several legislators are attending various academic programmes at the University of Liberia and other colleges around Monrovia. Schooling while making laws is no criminal offense. However, it renders them academically busy, thereby making them ineffective and inefficient. Even though the constitution places no educational limits on legislators, but it is obvious that illiterate and ignorant lawmakers in this technologically advanced global arena seem to pose more danger to democratic governance compared to well-educated and professional persons who better understand the dynamics of governance and the need to promote pro-poor public policies.

Additionally, the weakness and corrupt nature of the Legislature is that many lawmakers, prior to their election, do not have their own homes or houses in the Capital, Monrovia, which is the seat of government. Hence, they become preoccupied with settling down as opposed to accessing and addressing the needs of their constituents. The function of these problems is the promulgation of legislations that sideline the interests and aspirations of the citizens. Legislators create huge benefits for themselves, purchase flashy vehicles, extract humongous fees from concessionaires, make self-interested laws, and begin to live a high standard lifestyle far beyond the ordinary citizens whom they claim to represent. A case in point is that the current members of the 53rd Legislature earn not less than $13,000. USD in a country where the current poverty rate is 74.6% in rural areas, 47.7% in urban sectors and 61.5% average at the national level (LISGIS 2008). This simply means that while 61.5% of the population live below One US Dollar a day, they lawmakers earn $433.USD daily.

Admittedly, there has been some research done on this subject, but none has been able to point out the mean faults that lead to unabated presidential dominance and legislative dormancy, which deny the ordinary citizens greater access to their resources, and make them to mostly depend on the President for redress of their needs. Past researchers showed how lawmakers conduct legislative activities; make decisions on crucial state matters like emergencies and threat to peace, among others. But there has been no pointed research at the impact of poverty, greed, illiteracy, lack of transparency in budget process, and corruption on the balance of power in Liberia. This book therefore focuses on and delves into and analyses these factors, their impact on national growth and development due to weakness of the system of checks and balances. It suggests ways forward that may lead to the formulation of national policies and laws in the best interest of the suffering and impoverished majority.

Can the dormant Legislature assume its responsibilities to curb presidential dominance such that high political competition amongst citizens is focused on the Legislature rather than the presidency? What are Legislative responsibilities and how can the legislature assume them? What makes legislators weak and ineffective? What can be done to make lawmakers strong and effective? Finding answers to questions like these form the basis for writing this book.

1.2 The Need for this Book

There is a need to study and write about the performance and operations of the National Legislature of Liberia, especially in the post-conflict context. This will allow measurement of legislative efficiency against reemergence of presidential autocracy. Furthermore, this book is necessary because those elected to the Liberian Legislature do not adequately perform their duties as required by law. For instance, the Catholic Justice and Peace Commission monthly reports (2007) on the performance of the Legislature show that the 52nd Legislature spent more time bickering on the removal of a Speaker and advocating for increased benefits for themselves rather than enacting laws that would transform the lives of ordinary Liberians whom they "represent". Many lawmakers, according to the reports, were either absent from sessions or sat without proposing any law or bill, yet there are many public policy issues needing the rightful legislations. Many more were unable to articulate any view on the legislative process; yet they received their monthly allowances and benefits unhindered.

Several legislators do not frequently visit their constituencies to assess problems affecting those constituencies, needless talk about operating local offices within those constituencies or electoral districts. During their second sitting in 2007, the 52nd Legislature attempted to enact a financial autonomy bill that would grant it exclusive control of its allocated finances in the national budget. This bill sought to remove the Legislature from financial accountability and tax payments, but the President vetoed it. Also, due to their lack of effective and efficient oversight, almost all projects earmarked for constituencies in the national budgets of 2005/2006, 2006/2007, 2007/2008, 2008/2009, 2009/2010 and onwards were not successfully implemented. Notwithstanding, the National Legislature took no concrete steps to ensure the completion of such projects intended to develop the rural and underprivileged localities in the country.

The neglect of credible and pro-poor law making by legislators is not unique to this current one. The Legislature during President Taylor's regime failed to ratify major concessions that siphoned millions of dollars from the country. The Oriental Timber Company (OTC) that operated a multi-million-dollar business without the input of the members of the 51st Legislature is a classic case (UN Panel Report on Liberia, 2003). Members of the 51st Legislature requested President Sirleaf's administration to pay benefits that were owed them by the Taylor's regime when, indeed, they were the very legislators who ratified all national budgets for said tyrannical regime. The failure of lawmakers to have received their allocated salaries during the Taylor's autocratic regime portrays that constituents got nothing more than agony, suppression and misery from the operation of the 51st Legislature.

The 50th Legislature for its part failed to uphold Article 34 Section C of the constitution "authorizing it to declare war and conclude peace" (Liberia Constitution, 2000). It rejected peaceful negotiations with rebels and instructed President Doe to fight, using all resources available to him. The civil war, not prevented, led to the complete destruction of the state and its institutions. Today, government is struggling with the reconstruction of the infrastructure and state institutions of the Republic of Liberia.

The current legislators still enact pro-elitist laws to protect the interest of the minority elites. This book is therefore important because it discusses why lawmakers do not work in the interests of those who elect them, and why the President is so powerful in the face of a dependent Judiciary. It suggests what could be done to remedy the situation. It is also very important because the Executive Branch enjoys enormous powers over the Judiciary due to the weakness of the latter. It is therefore essential to unearth the reasons responsible for a weak Judiciary, analyze them and posit a way forward to curtailing executive dominance in the country.

1.3 Assumptions Regarding the Problem of Checks and Balance in Liberia

Legislative inefficiency and ineffectiveness nurture presidential autocracy that in turn breeds unreasonable avarice and competition for the position of President in Liberia. It denies the people their right to good governance, which normally derives from checks and balances largely dependent on the objective performance of lawmakers. As a result, the mass citizens suffer while government officials, including legislators, flourish at the people's detriment. This problem hampers national growth and development; thus, it is important to remedy it. If the national government must protect the national interest (provide for the security and wellbeing of its people), it is imperative that lawmakers perform their duties and responsibilities diligently, objectively and honestly. To have checks and balances amongst the three branches of government, the legislators must not chase wealth or aspire for elitist stature that drives them to breaking the very laws they enact. When legislators enact laws that will alleviate the poverty and suffering of the people whom they theoretically represent in Liberia, there could be national stability, good governance, peace, economic growth, infrastructural development, and societal transformation.

More so, if the electorates scrutinize aspirants for the legislature and elect individuals with consistent record of advocacy for positive change, high academic standard, candidates who are well knowledgeable, transparent and development oriented, etc., good laws could be formulated and enacted without compromise. And if the civil society enlightens and empowers the citizens on the governance process, rule of law, and hold government accountable, the people would largely vote right, intelligibly and ultimately hold their government accountable.

The analysis and findings in this study would eventually lead to a crude awakening of the citizens, civil society and the legislators themselves. Such awakening would then eventually lead to a participatory populace, aggressive civil society, an unbiased and responsible judiciary and an effective and objective Legislature that would transform the society through good legislations.

1.4 Scope and Limitation of this Book

This book focuses the coordination amongst the three branches of the Liberian government, namely (1) The Legislature; (2) The Executive; and (3) The Judiciary. It discusses the balance of power amongst the three branches. It urges and challenges the overbearing and imperial presidency, dominating the Legislature, to play by the rules of checks and balances. It does not exhaust all discussions and concepts about Liberian Government and Politics. It first historicizes the etymology of political parties and analyzes the dynamics of balance of power from 1847 to present. It does not pedantically cover all the actions of the Legislature and Executive or Judiciary since independence, but rather draws from carefully selected historical highlights that are used as yard stick to rationalize and conceptualize the defects and lapses of the principles of checks and balances enshrined in the Constitution, thus resulting in an ineffective and lackadaisical Legislature. Due to the April 12, 1980 coup d'état, there were intermittent formulations of transitional legislatures; however, they are not discussed because they all were extra-constitutional.

The book is further limited to the politics of the Republic of Liberia, although its findings could be used in and applied to other countries' contexts to analyze the balance of power amongst branches of government and make inferences or conclusions. It only considers factors responsible for a weak Legislature, powerful Presidency, lukewarm Judiciary, and what can be done to remedy the situation so that laws made are in the best interest of the people. This consideration is found in Chapter Five where an analysis of a sample survey conducted on the campus of the University of Liberia during the author's graduate research can be found. Lastly, I have discussed some prospects and challenges facing national government and analyzed the role of the international community in the ongoing national policy formulation and implementation. This last part is important because, without the intervention of the international community, Liberia could have still been at war as was between 1989 and 2003; hence, the need to highlight the role of the International system in Liberia's democracy.

1.5 Chapter One Summary

Liberia, founded by freed slaves from the United States of America in 1822, got her independence on 26 July 1847. The formation of the nation-state by the minority group, the settlers, placed political and economic power in the hands of an oligarchic controlled legislative, executive and judicial authority as "The Leading Citizens" during the nineteenth century (Sawyer 1992).

Although this leading oligarchy cherished the nineteenth century democratic values bordering on the separation of powers through checks and balances, subsequent generations, evolving from the settler minority and ascending to power in the early parts of the 20th century, betrayed the concept of checks and balances, engendered autocratic tendencies in the Executive and trampled on the Legislature and the Judiciary.

On 27 September 1847 when the first constitution of the Republic of Liberia was approved at the special election or referendum, the very first Legislature comprising six Senators (two each from Montserrado, Bassa and Sinoe), eight Representatives (four from Montserrado, three from Bassa, and one from Sinoe) were elected (Guannu, 2000). This first Legislature worked in consonance with the first President of the State, Joseph Jenkins Roberts, who appointed his political rival and President of the First Constitutional Convention, Samuel Benedict, as the first Chief Justice.

It can be deduced that checks and balances were bound to abound because this new government comprised eligible, hardworking, experienced and fastidious men who declared the first republic on the African continent; and whose ambition was to let the world know that black people could govern themselves. The appointment of an opposition leader as Chief Justice was also an indication of the fact that the government upheld the principle of inclusion and checks and balances, especially by establishing an independent Judiciary. It is far from reality in contemporary Liberia for an opposition leader to be appointed to the Bench of the Supreme Court fearing that such act would lead to a non-conformist and independent Judiciary. Perhaps the time is near for such repeat of history.

Unarguably, the first Legislature and succeeding legislatures up to 1943 were mostly effective due to several factors. One, they had a shorter tenure of office; thus, they were obliged to perform better or risk removal and or forfeit re-election if they poorly performed. For instance, prior to 1907, Senators only stayed in office for four years, while Representatives were elected for two years (Guannu 2000). They had to be effective to be re-elected and or leave a legacy that would opportune them to ascend to other positions, including the presidency. Two, these legislators were virtually literate, and they were either businessmen who accrued their own wealth as well as brought experience from the private sector. Sometimes, some were descendants, children or in-laws of former politicians. Thus, they had experience and were independent of the executive or knew the workings of the state prior to their ascendancy. Also, many of the lawmakers, as stated earlier, had either worked in the Judiciary or Executive, thereby enhancing their capacities to making good laws. One of the basic misgivings of the legislature prior to 1943 was that the indigenous majority was not represented, or if they were, then it was by error or chance.

The culture of presidential dominance took root in Liberia during the rule of Tubman. Tubman was the first president to come from outside of either Montserrado or Bassa County. These two counties produced all the country's presidents since independence, excluding President William V.S. Tubman of Maryland, Samuel Kanyon Doe of Grand Gedeh, and Moses Z. Blah of Nimba and Ellen Johnson-Sirleaf of Bomi. Tubman created Grand Gedeh, Lofa, Bong, and Nimba counties in 1964 when he dissolved the provinces. This gesture was, in part, due to international condemnation for pseudo colonialism and to woo the indigenes support for his unabated quest for the presidency. The new counties and districts created by Tubman were controlled by his stooges. Lawmakers therefrom were also handpicked under his influence by the ruling True Whig Party that he fought so hard to dominate amidst his Bassa and Montserrado contenders and compatriots. More besides, Tubman had accrued so much wealth, which he used to lure the legislators and judicial workers into submissions.

CHAPTER II

VIEWS OF OTHER SCHOLARS

In *'Making Democracy work in Liberia, the Constitution'*, Wagner (2000) asserts that when groups of people create a constitution, they prescribe their desired form of government. In this regard, the Liberian constitution prescribes a republican government for Liberians. This form of government allows the people to elect their leaders who must account to them. In other words, Liberia practices indirect democracy otherwise known as representative democracy. Unlike other forms of government wherein leaders suppress the governed (autocracy, dictatorship, tyranny, etc.), the constitution gives the people the right under the republican form of government to remove their leaders from power if their (people's) safety and happiness demands; but such must be in accordance with procedures laid down in the same constitution (Liberia Constitution 1986). It accords limits on all branches of government to forestall any dominating others. His analysis fits the purpose of this book because under the republican form of government, no one branch of government is to overshadow others in whatever manner and form. Equally, he simplifies the entire Constitution of Liberia thus making it easier for the highly illiterate population to grasp its contents and to know what their lawmakers and other branches of government ought to and ought not to do.

Sawyer (1992) argues in the *'Emergence of Autocracy in Liberia: Tragedy and Challenge'* that the settlers adopted an alien constitution that didn't accommodate the traditional practices of the indigenous majority, but they managed to affect a western model of democracy – republicanism – which disallows autocracy. Howbeit, the settlers built a "civilized society", but their descendents introduced executive dominance in the early twentieth century. This, according to him, facilitated military dictatorship and ubiquitous conflict in the century. Sawyer views presidential autocracy as a result of the then rigid constitutional limits of centralized authority imposed by an "alien" constitution of 1847, which centralized power in the laps of a few unaccountable to the majority. The centralized authority, he maintains, flourished amidst a weak economy, the absence of the rule of law, and the exclusion of the tribal majority. Sawyer specifically places the apex of domineering Executive at the feet of Tubman who entrenched himself in power, became an autonomous Presidential boss, and made the presidency sovereign. The analysis of Dr Sawyer is quiet in place because in the first instance a republican government is not supposed to accommodate autocratic tendencies; but there is a plethora of evidence of autocratic tendencies in Liberia.

Additionally, the early part of the First Republic marginalized the indigenous majority by excluding them from participation in decision-making, entrenching the crises of distribution, participation and not working adequately to resolve the crisis of identity, etc. However, legislators during the zenith of the settlers' rule were more effective and efficient up to the Tubman era when this trend was reversed. The high illiteracy amongst the natives, mass poverty, corruption, greed and scramble for wealth by the privileged few who managed to infiltrate the established settler oligarchy helped to betray the lofty ideals of republican democracy; hence further suppressing the majority. Now that the settler-native divide seems far remote owing to an increased involvement of many indigenous in national decision making, there is a need to have political reformation that will place credible, literate, rational, nationalistic and objective natives in the national Legislature to serve the best interests of the suffering masses by making transformative laws.

Wreh (1976) critically analyzes Tubman as a man who made himself a personal dictator. His *'Love of Liberty'* states that there existed no countervailing force from the people, civil society or the Legislature and Judiciary to neutralize Tubman's autocracy. He accounts for Tubman's amassment of wealth at the disadvantage of the state – a situation that promoted Tubman's patronage system and 'presidential cultism'. Moreover, he gives adequate accounts of Tubman's systematic oppression of oppositions. Tubman cleverly manipulated the other branches of government and established a cartel of family members in key government functionaries, among others. Tubman's formulation of diverse security units just to keep him protected did not escape the memories of Wreh who himself felt the pains of the regime's brutality. In *'The Love of Liberty'*, Wreh (1976) provides further support for the claim made earlier that the domineering presidency germinated under the aegis of Tubman.

In a related manner, Liebenow's (1987 & 1970) respective books *'Liberia, the Quest for Democracy'*, and *'Liberia, the Evolution of Privilege'* further elaborate that Liberia's republican democracy took shape, but later crumbled. Discussing the "Liberia's Paradox", he explains that the freed slaves segregated against in the New World returned home (in Liberia, Africa) to enjoy liberty, but in turn marginalized and suppressed the indigenous. The paradox is that those who were suppressed and later liberated returned "home" and in turn suppressed the natives. They also frowned on their new home (Liberia) and considered North America their original home as was enshrined in the Preamble of the Constitution of the First Republic (Liberia Constitution 1847).

Moreover, Liebenow clarifies that the minority elites adopted a western democratic model, which honored the republican form like that of the United States of America; nevertheless, these settlers discriminated against the tribal groups, thereby betraying the ideals of republicanism.

He maintains, and I concur, that instead of a system of checks and balances, power concentrated in the hands of a caste of "colonial" minority through the Executive branch in which the indigenous found it difficult to be represented. Under these socio-political and economically exclusionary policies, the 1980 widely acclaimed coup d'etat ended the minority rule, but produced another dictator, Samuel Kanyon Doe. The quest for democracy continued even under the Doe regime that ascended to power through unconstitutional means. This quest for democracy still goes on in Liberia.

'The American Political System' (Melusky 2000) is one of the basic texts for discussing republican democracy. He argues that direct democracy is not possible in a country with a larger population. Therefore, indirect democracy or a republican democracy remains a possibility. He further asserts that in this form of democracy, the citizens are sovereign (Mulusky 2000). Melusky speaks of popular sovereignty as a keystone in the context of democratic thinking. Under popular sovereignty, the people have "absolute power". They give authority to a group of selected or elected persons to lead and control a government; however, the question of accountability to the people remains fundamental'.

Melusky analyzes the operations of the American political system placing the Congress in a pivotal position. He argues that Legislators, presidents, judges, and all those in the bureaucracy of government do not own the political system, but rather it is the people who own it. And the direct representatives of the owners (people) are the Congress that, in the case of Liberia, is the Legislature. This posits that for democracy to work well, the people who are owners of the political system must ensure that their leaders, mainly the Legislature, remain accountable to them. The people must also ensure that good and progressive laws are made by petitioning their law makers.

His book examines the ways through which the people can hold political leaders responsible. It also defines the functions of the three branches of the United States Government. And since Liberia borrowed America's political model, it is fair to use the American experience in analyzing the balance of power in Liberia. Melusky's work really provides an ideal comparative model of republican democracy, which this study endeavors to analyze in the context of the Republic of Liberia.

CHAPTER III

EMREGENCE OF POLITICAL PARTIES IN LIBERIA

1.1 Background:

Liberia, founded by free slaves from North America through the instrumentality of the American Colonization Society (ACS), was established in 1822. The state was a colony between 1822 and 1839. It became a commonwealth from 1839-1847. By July 26, 1847, the colony turned commonwealth became an independent country, thereby making it the first Republican sovereign state on the African continent.

The First Republic, which lasted from 1847 to 1980 in Liberian history was mostly peaceful in view of the absence of a full-scale civil war, though there were systemic forms of social-cultural, political and economic violence bordered on marginalization, suppression and bad governance. This period witnessed the transfer of power amongst the settler groups, thus totally marginalizing the indigenous majority. The conduct of governance relative to participation was highly exclusive; hence culminating into the violent overthrow of the government in 1980 by the military. The proclaimed basis of the military overthrow was marginalization of the indigenous and widespread corruption by the dethroned regime. The coup makers, having come from ethnic backgrounds, dissolved and or suspended the constitution of the first Republic, which did not promote multiparty democracy to its fullest. Thus, in 1986, a new constitution was established and adopted. This 1986 constitution, in Chapter VIII, Article 77a states that:

> Since the essence of democracy is free competition of ideas expressed by political parties and political groups as well as by individuals, parties may freely be established to advocate the political opinions of the people. Laws, regulations, decrees or measures which might have the effect of creating a one-party state shall be declared unconstitutional.

1.2 Multipartism in Liberia in Retrospect

Multiparty democracy was highly illusive in the political history of Liberia up to the years of President William R. Tolbert to whom credit is given for the advent of multiparty democracy in Liberia (Travers 2005). The history of Liberia between 1822 and 1847 is what I commonly refer to as "Liberia's formative historic period". By 1822, the settlers had arrived at Providence Island, thereby marking the foundation of the modern state of Liberia. From 1822 to 1839 the ACS administered the 'State" as a Colony headed by Colonial Agents. By 1839, the Colony was transformed into a Commonwealth, which brought together Baxley, Bassa Cove and Montserrado. The Colony and Commonwealth, headed by agents and a governor, respectively, did not practice party politics. Liberia was not colonized because, in the sense of the term, a colony must be presided over by sovereign power. Hence in the Liberia-ACS relation, the ACS was a philanthropic religious organization whose main agenda was to return free blacks to Africa and Christianize what was then termed "the Dark Continent".

The question of who became president after independence was paramount to the newly declared state. To answer this question, two fronts or parties were established, hence the emergence of party politics in Liberia. The Pro-Administration or True Liberian Party was headed by Joseph Jenkins

Roberts, while the Anti-Administration or Whig Party put forth Samuel Benedict. JJ Roberts was the last governor of the Commonwealth. Hence, his emergence as Standard-Bearer gave rise to the nomenclature, 'Pro-Administration', and was a symbol of power perpetuation. Anti-Administration meant those opposed to JJ Roberts' continued stay in power. Samuel Benedict led the Anti-Administration group under the Whig Party. The True Liberian Party versus the Whig Party marked the evolution of political parties in the Republic of Liberia. The True Liberian Party comprised mulattoes/light-skin settlers, and the Whigs were predominantly dark-skin settlers. As such, the political competition took the trend of skin pigmentation. Skin pigmentation or race became the *Modus Operandi* of the state up to 1877 when Anthony W. Gardner, a dark-skin Liberian, of the opposition TWP, a dark-skin Liberian, defeated James Springs Payne of the mulattoes (Guannu 2005).

There was the formation of intermittent political parties throughout this period, but without much to achieve in the practice of multiparty democracy. For instance, the dark-skin Liberians in 1860 founded the True Whig Party. This party, with Edward J. Roye as its Standard-Bearer defeated the Republican Party of the ruling mulatto elites. Resentment between the settlers based on skin color made party politics vindictive. This led to the forceful removal of E.J. Roye in 1871 (Guannu 2005) and subsequent impeachment of Vice President James Smith who ended Roye's tenure but is not considered a former President of Liberia in the recorded presidential history of the country.

Political power and participation remained in the hands of one group from 1847 up to 1946 when the "Act to regulate all Elections in the Republic of Liberia" lifted the disenfranchisement of natives, but with property limitation (Wreh 1976). Even with the conditional franchise given to the natives, party politics obtained amongst the settler elites, leaving out the indigenes who were generally illiterate.

The 1885 elections referred to as the first multiparty elections (Guannu 2005) did not witness the participation of indigenous candidates. Subsequently, the 1931 elections between Edwin Barclay's TWP and his Secretary of Treasury's People's Party, as well as the elections of May 1943 between TWP's William V.S. Tubman and Democratic Party's James F. Cooper did not feature indigenous candidates. So were the controversial elections of 1955 between Tubman and Barclay (Wreh 1976). However, these elections had more than one party competing. Contrastingly, it was the 1951 elections of Tubman and Didheo Tweh that first involved an indigenous (Wreh 1976). The True Whig Party of Tubman denied the massive indigenous-based United People's Party registration then led by Tweh. Thus, Tweh joined the Reformation Party whose campaign agents were later arrested and detained by the incumbent president Tubman's security apparatus in Bassa and other areas (Wreh 1976).

On the average, party politics during this period witnessed terror, marginalization, and bans from then incumbent leaders. The political terrain was occasioned by competition between either two parties, which could preferable be termed a period of bipartisanship. Therefore, it can be concluded that multiparty democracy, which is characterized by many political parties that are highly competitive, did not actually exist fully. However, the ascendancy of President William R Tolbert, Jr. brought a new chapter in the history of multipartism in Liberia. Consequently, this historic epoch can be considered the evolution of multipatism as earlier stated. President Tolbert in the 1970s indulged in the political liberalization of the Republic. For instance, in 1973 the Movement for Justice in Africa (MOJA) was founded. Later MOJA had a political offspring, the Liberia People's Party. In the same vein, the Progressive Alliance of Liberia (PAL) got organized in 1975, giving birth to the Progressive People's Party (PPP) that later transformed into the United People's Party (UPP).

Both MOJA and PAL advocated variety of political ideologies, as well as social and economic changes in Liberia. Their emergence on the political stage with their offshoots (LPP and UPP) raised political consciousness amongst the indigenous masses. It is believed that Tolbert's liberal political philosophy offended the ruling elitist True Whig Partisans. Concurrently, some critics hold the view that Tolbert's shift from the traditional political bossism led to his hasty demise. Yet, others believe that the liberalism of Tolbert to allow open political opposition without a structured mechanism to control such free political competition resulted into unintended consequences and an untimely overthrow of his government in 1980 by the indigenous military. Here, the first Republic ended giving rise to the Second Republic.

On 12 April 1980, seventeen non-commissioned officers of the Armed Forces of Liberia (AFL) overthrew President Tolbert and assassinated him. The Military junta, named and styled the People's Redemption Council (PRC), suspended the 1847 Constitution. This junta presided over the state using decrees, some of which banned political activities of any form. There were no party politics from 1980-1984 when the PRC transformed itself into the Interim National Assembly (INA) (Guanu 2005). The INA incorporated civilians in the running of the state, lifted bans on political parties and transformed itself into a political party, the National Democratic Party of Liberia (NDPL). The NDPL, UPP, LPP, the Liberia Action Party (LAP), the Liberia Unification Party (LUP), and the Unity Party (UP) paraded the corridor of politics. Multipartism seemed to have reached its apex. However, synonymous to the tradition of politics in the first Republic, the INA banned both UPP and LPP prior to the 1985 elections. In addition, it placed political and legal barriers on LAP, LUP and UP, thus making the NDPL the victor in the 1985 elections. Later, it was alleged that the NDPL rigged the elections to maintain the military turned politicians in power. Some analysts believe that NDPL acted in the interest of the indigenous majority to disallow the eventual return of the settlers' minority disguised under the formidable banner of the Liberia Action Party (LAP) but others disagree.

Just as the elections of 1885 and 1927 were occasioned by claims of vote rigging and discontentment on the part of "defeated" parties, disenchanted opposition parties formed the Grand Coalition to protest the 1985 elections results. Mr Samuel Doe used military power to suppress the opposition, thereby undermining the spirit and intent of multiparty democracy in the Republic of Liberia. The seed of discord was then further fertilized, increasing tensions between the indigenous and settlers on the one hand, and amongst the indigenous majority themselves on the other. The blatant disregard for the political freedoms guaranteed under Article 77 of the constitution as evidenced by the banning, strangulation of opposition parties, and the establishment of political bottlenecks in the country invited a new political terrain. All that occasioned the terror and horror of the Samuel Doe's regime is now history, but this period initiated the transformation of arm bandits into politicians, an act that would later haunt Liberia.

The National Patriotic Front of Liberia (NPFL) intervened in Liberian politics under the banner of "Freedom Fighters". History has however indicated that this was a mere fallacy as the so-called freedom fighters and their rivals maimed, and killed over 250,000 people during the 14 years of civil conflict. However, the NPFL's invasion of 24 December 1989 was welcomed by many Liberians owing to Samuel Doe's autocratic rule. The rebel incursion of 24 December 1989 delved a significant blow in the working and practices of multiparty democracy in Liberia. It was very certain that the Samuel Doe's government would have held elections in 1991, but the civil hostilities disallowed elections to proceed as planned. The control of the state changed hands between and amongst rival warring factions. The late President Doe accused exiled and disgruntled politicians of backing the insurgence in order to disrupt the 1991 elections in which the ten-year constitutional clause could have prohibited their participation (Youboty 2004).

The civil war of 1989 lasted up to 1997 when, on 19 July 1997, elections were conducted by the Independent Elections Commission of Liberia. These elections saw the participation of thirteen political parties. Once again, multipartism had resurfaced with the former rebel leader Charles Taylor emerging as the 21st President of the Republic of Liberia. Once again, armed factions repeated history by transforming themselves into political parties for political competition. Cases in point include, but not limited to the transformations of the National Patriotic Front (NPFL) into the National Patriotic Party (NPP)-winner of the 1997 elections, and United Liberation Movement (UNLIMO) into the All Liberian Coalition Party (ALCOP), etc.

Bad governance as well as widespread abuse of human rights sprang up under the 2 August 1997 newly installed government. Political oppositions, including this writer, were oppressed, suppressed, beaten by armed men and on several occasions jailed. In fact, opposition parties from the 1997 elections were predominantly excluded from the government. However, some of the parties later collaborated with the NPP. In the wake of simmering opposition politics under the NPP led government, the first social democratic political party of Liberia was organized in 1999. This new party was the New Democratic Alternative for Liberia's Movement (The New DEAL Movement). Additionally, the Liberty Party also evolved. These two political parties bravely challenged the ruling NPP on critical national issues and kept the government in check amidst ubiquitous militarization of the state and unmatched brutality of the security apparatus.

Despite the fearless political posture of the new parties, there was mass exodus of opposition figures into exile; hence, the stage was set for renewed civil war in the country. One thing that should be emphasized is that for the second time in the country's history, a political party formed out of an arm group won elections and ran yet another autocratic and dictatorial regime. This was the National Patriotic Party (NPP), NDPL being the first. Two years later under the rule of the NPP, a renewed rebel incursion by the Liberians United for Reconciliation and Democracy (LURD) occurred in Lofa County. Just as the NPFL, LURD cited bad governance, corruption, crackdown on political oppositions and the abuse of human right as reasons for the insurgency. This new civil strife was exacerbated by the entry through Grand Gedeh County of another arm group, the Movement for Democracy in Liberia (MODEL). MODEL was mainly of the Krahn ethnic allies to the late Samuel Kanyon Doe, though this faction had other tribal elements within its ranks and file.

Multipartism once more was strangulated. Negotiations in Accra, Ghana to end this round of war gave rise to the National Transitional Government of Liberia-NTGL (Accra Comprehensive Peace Agreement 2003). The NTGL was headed by members of political parties, rebel factions, civil society and political subdivisions. Chairman Charles G. Bryant and his Deputy Wesley Johnson came from the LAP and UPP, respectively. The National Transitional Legislative Assembly (NTLA) had its composition from political parties, counties, rebel groups and the civil society. The various ministries, autonomous agencies and corporations were also divided amongst said groups. It is good to note that this was the first time political parties in the country, after overtly participating in negotiations to end the war, became head of the negotiated government. The Civil Society was notably allotted seven slots in the National Transitional Legislative Assembly (NTLA) and several other positions in government.

The two-year rule of the NTGL opened the corridor for the October 2005 elections. Those elections were contested by 22 candidates from various parties and independent candidates. Prior to these elections, the National Elections Commission put the number of registered political parties at a little over 30. This attests to the fact that multiparty democracy resurfaced in grand style; but this time without any ruling party's absolute control of the political system. However, it is worthy of note that most of these political parties were not and still are not institutionalized. They are centered on individuals, thus undermining the actual spirit and intent of political institutions as stated in Article 77 of the Constitution. While political leaders are to blame on the one hand for weak political parties, members of the parties and the National Elections Commission are also to blame on the other because they fail to hold party leaders accountable based on the rules governing political parties in the country.

The 2005 elections ended in a second round between the footballer George Weah led Congress for Democratic Change (CDC) which toke first place in the first round, and the Ellen Johnson-Sirleaf led Unity Party (UP) that came second in the first round. Interestingly, the Unity Party won the elections amidst widespread accusation of massive electoral fraud and manipulations initiated by the Elections Commission, then headed by Cllr. Frances Johnson-Morris, cousin to Madam Ellen Johnson-Sirleaf. The rising tensions from the controversial elections were thwarted by the United Nations Mission in Liberia. Some political pundits pointed accusing fingers to the United Nations for favoring Madam Sirleaf for the Presidency, thereby helping her win the elections. This has yet to be proven by verifiable evidence. There were mass demonstrations by supporters of the CDC, but the party leadership abandoned its vote rigging claims in lieu of negotiations brokered by the International Contact Group on Liberia (ECOWAS, MRU, AU, EU, UN, USA, etc.). Mr Weah unilaterally withdrew his vote rigging claim from the Supreme Court. This brought him under serious criticism as taking bribe from either the international community or the ruling Unity Party. Again, these claims are yet to be validated independently.

Since the formation of the State in 1822 and its independence in 1847, no form of multipartism had produced the composition of government that came out of the 2005 elections. The ruling

Unity Party (UP) had a negligible number of legislators in the House of Representatives and the Liberian Senate. Majority of the Legislators came from defeated political parties at the presidential level. Hence, the Senate and the House of Representatives used their strength as opposition to block several policies implementation by the Executive. For instance, the Legislature amended the Act creating the National Port Authority, making its budget subservient to the National Legislature. This move was laudable, yet insufficient as there are several other government agencies and institutions that manage state resources without effective oversight from the Legislature. The Legislature, instead of fostering national unity, peace and development, has been bent on trivialities that would blackmail the Liberia political system. It appears these opposition forces longed to settle political scores with the victor of the 2005 elections ignoring the essence of national coherence. There has been a consistent undermining of national development and reunification at the detriment of the suffering majority. On the reverse, the Executive adopts an aristocratic posture over the Legislature that is predominantly composed of mediocre individuals, former combatants and corrupt government officials of past regimes.

Multiparty democracy in Liberia is not based on ideological differences. It is rather tailored along the ballooning interests of political bosses pursuing either their selfish interest or to have them accommodated in National Government. Multiparty politics in Liberia sometimes promote ethnic or regional cleavages at the detriment of national unity. Ethnicity played a major role in the further creation of counties in the country. The formation of counties in Liberia of recent was based on tribal segments or interest of marginalized groups. River Gee, Rivercess, Grand Kru, Gbarpolu, and Margibi are classic examples.

The formation of political parties is also taking similar trends. During the 2005 and 2011 elections, voters voted on tribal lines as were the cases of Charles Brumskin winning land slide in

Bassa, George Weah in several parts of the South East and slump communities in urban areas where southeasterners, mainly the Kru, are based, Cllr. Varney Sherman's overwhelming victory in Grand Cape Mount, and Dr Joseph Kortu's 2005 popular vote in Nimba, and Prince Johnson's 2011 overwhelming vote in Nimba, which placed him in third place amongst presidential candidates. All these candidates and many others overwhelmingly won in their counties and or regions of origin. This emerging ethnic voting in national elections is worrying and needs to attract the attention of national government, especially in promoting peace and reconciliation amongst the people of Liberia. Ethnicity was one of the key drivers of the barbaric 14-year civil war in Liberia. Therefore, and all efforts should be made to discourage the re-emergence of ethnic cleavages in national politics.

3.3 Summary

This chapter has discussed the evolution of multiparty democracy in Liberia. There was nothing like party politics in Liberia from 1822 to 1847. From 1847 to 1980, party politics was illusive because political contest was based in the hands of the minority settlers' hegemony. This period witnessed one-party dominance if not monopartism. Even though political liberalization took shape during the rule of President Tolbert, multiparty democracy was actualized in the 1980s, but was undermined by the fraudulent elections of 1985 and banning of opposition parties (Kaydor, unpublished undergraduate thesis 2002). Settlers' elitism, socio-political, economic and ethnic discrimination led to the violent coup d'etat in 1980. The electoral fraud, coupled with political grievance from the rule of the PRC and INA turned NDPL, prompted the aborted 12 November 1985 Thomas Quinwonkpa led invasion. That invasion paved the road to the 24 December 1989 rebel incursion. The notorious conduct of the civil war, which occasioned the formation of several rival warring factions, further ruined the development of multiparty democracy in Liberia.

Although the 1997 elections seemingly restored multiparty democracy, political marginalization and intolerance retarded its growth. Howbeit, the advent of the NTGL and the presence of the United Nations Mission in Liberia (UNMIL) helped to restore multiparty politics in Liberia. Currently, the national government has a conglomeration of officials from diverse political backgrounds, making it difficult to have an unanimity of interest in fostering a positive national agenda. It is the responsibility of the public officials to mirror themselves as Liberians, not opposition politicians. This would help harness the re-construction, development, growth and transformation of the war-ravaged nation-state, Liberia. Notwithstanding, it is equally important for political institutions to be objective and critical of government policies based on national interest. Opposition political parties should not only criticize government policies; they must propose alternative measures to overcome national problems. They also need to pressure their legislators to advocate for and formulate laws that mirror the alternative agenda of opposition parties. Such laws need to be people-centered and progressive, rather than selfish and retrogressive.

CHAPTER IV

CHECKS AND BALANCES (1847-PRESENT)

4.1 The Legislature and Executive (1847-1980)

Legislative authority was indistinguishable from the authority of the President with his cabinet, former Presidents, influential merchants, and the ruling party in the early parts of the 18th and 19th centuries (Liebenow 1987). Indistinguishable because the ruling parties, initially the Republican and later the Whigs, were the camouflage decision markers of the entire government. In conjunction with the "leading citizen's council" (a consortium of ex-government officials and eminent citizens), the party performed legislative duties. Such practice had no legal standing, yet decisions emanating therefrom were binding on the state. Howbeit, the Legislators were offsprings of the political order; thus, they were not bothered by its modus operandi.

The political syndicate (president, ministers, and ex-presidents, influential merchants, the Legislature, judicial workers and the party) was the final authority in times of national crisis and decision making. For instance, President Anthony W. Gardiner resigned under pressure from this group in 1883 owing to border conflict with colonial territories of Great Britain. President William David Coleman forcibly abdicated office in 1900 due to his "controversial" interior policies that ignited the Gola hostilities. Similarly, with pressure from the same body, President Daniel E. Howard convened a meeting to resolve the German bombing affairs in 1914 (Sawyer 1992). President Charles D.B. King was impeached in relation to his involvement with slavery and forced labor in 1930, due to international intervention and pressure. The Masonic Craft was another powerful source of decision making. It decided government officials' appointment, retention or removal. The decisions taken at fraternal gatherings were automatically binding on the state.

The foregoing analysis point to several issues. First, the operation of government outside the constitutional structures; second, international intervention to resolve internal political rivalries. And third, the Legislature was a rubber stamp as election of legislators, just as the president, was based either on consensus or nomination from the ruling party, fraternal identity, and the political elites. For example, Tubman ascended to the Senate at age 28 instead of 30, the required age then; thus, depicting the political manipulation that characterized the state (Wreh 1976). He served the Legislature, the Judiciary and later became the Head of State. He therefore mastered the tricks, dealings and manipulations of the political system. Political hell broke loose when Tubman assumed the Presidency. He "packed the Legislature with his servants, cronies and favorites, many of them illiterate; others were his social secretaries, others his chauffeur and valet or wards" (Wreh 1976). He introduced recruitment of indigenous in the Legislature. This act brought about indigenous peoples' participation in governance, but those recruited were practically unfit to articulate the interests of their constituents. He controlled and bullied them. Hence, the Legislature, like those prior to Tubman, was a toothless bulldog.

President Tolbert was Representative during the rule of Tubman. He later became Vice President to Tubman for nineteen unbroken years. He was caught in a dilemma of breaking with the past and preserving the status quo. Therefore, he did not make fundamental amendments to have instituted the principles of separation of power or checks and balances. He equally maintained the role of 'Masonic Craft' in the country's governance. However, Tolbert instituted some radical changes. He closely aligned with indigenous Liberians, respected their cultures, and liberalized the political terrain by allowing multiparty system. Tolbert introduced Kpelleh as a national language and ensured it was taught at the University of Liberia, but this was not legislated; hence. Liberia still lacks a local national language thereby making English the only official language. Despite these radical moves, the Legislature was his footstool. His older brother, Frank Tolbert, was President Pro Tempore of the Senate and became the most powerful Senator in the country. His younger brother, Stephen Tolbert was Finance Minister; and his son A.B. Tolbert was Representative, and Chair of the House Committee on Foreign Affairs, while other relatives or in-laws occupied key government posts. Cronyism, nepotism and favoritism were entrenched under his regime.

This period had a mixed picture of the Legislature. From 1847 to 1943, the Legislature was more robust, efficient, effective and powerful. Its effectiveness waned after President Tubman ascended to the presidency when he packed the Legislature with his cronies. After Tubman's rule, the reliance of the Legislature on the Executive continues unabated. Will the Legislature assume its constitutional responsibility and check the abuse of power by the Executive and Judiciary? History will be the best judge.

4.2 The Judiciary (1847-1980)

The Judiciary has a minute influence in Liberia as compared to the Legislature. It was very much the third branch of government. Inferior in the nineteenth century, its functions were limited to the mere interpretation of law and the constitution, settling disputes mostly involving low social status individuals (Liebenow 1989). The judiciary was largely made up of apprentice lawyers. By and large, the judiciary became a key collaborator with the Executive and legitimized the actions of the Executive. It also lacked the capacity to assert itself in dispensing justice, equity and fair play, but mostly indulged in the collection of fines that were often unaccounted for. For instance, in 1966, A. Dash Wilson, a former Chief Justice, announced that the collection of fines by judicial officials had resulted in a flagrant distortion of justice and proposed that judges turn this function over to administrative officers (Liebenow 1969).

Moreover, judges and justices were randomly removed. Tubman removed Justice Barclay for hearing Edwin Barclay's case on the fraudulent 1955 results of Presidential election. Impeachment of justices or judges by joint resolutions of the Legislature was widespread. In 1957 two Supreme Court judges were removed without cause (Liebenow 1987). In 2008 Magistrate Milton Taylor of the Monrovia City Court was illegally removed by the Executive; this was a violation of the Constitution of Liberia. Delays in prosecution of cases were another area of weakness on the part of the Judiciary. For example, in 1960 only seven cases out of 1,297 were tried within one-year period by the First Judicial Circuit Court in Montserrado County (Liebenow 1987). Several inmates languished in prison for indefinite periods. Today, several cases remain on courts' dockets, and several alleged criminals remain behind bars for months and years without being tried for crimes they have been accused of. These practices amounted to and still constitute the abuse of the fundamental rights and civil liberties of those accused of crimes and detained beyond the statutory time limit.

4.3 The Legislature (1985-Present)

The Second Republic witnessed accusations of fraudulent electoral process in 1985. President Doe's National Democratic Party (NDPL) accordingly rigged the elections, gave his party an overwhelming victory in the Presidential and General Elections in which he eked out 50.9% among four Presidential candidates, "won" 21 of the 26 seats in the Senate, and 51 of the 64 seats in the House of Representatives. The ninety-four seat bicameral Legislature had eighteen (18) legislators as opposition partisans, though one of the oppositions (Ms Ellen Johnson Sirleaf of the Liberia Action Party) refused to take the Senate seat based on the mandate from her party, and her personal disagreement with the outcome of the presidential elections in 1985 (Youboty 2003).

High rate of tribalism, ignorance and nepotism occasioned that regime. These factors, coupled with massive corruption and greed irrigated by emotions from the fraudulent 1985 elections, "justified" a rebel war on 24 December 1989 by Charles Taylor. Many Liberians welcomed the civil war due to Doe's autocracy. Presidential autocracy in the Second Republic was not opposed by the Legislature, then controlled by members of the ruling National Democratic Party of Liberia (NDPL) members. The Legislature could have, in the interest of the indigenous majority, changed the archaic, bias, and discriminatory laws enacted by the old regime. But to the dismay of the indigenes, the over 95% indigenous-dominated Legislature kept the old laws on the books and thrived on the spoils of the old political system. They instead enacted such laws like the laughable "Agricultural Break" that kept them out of office for six months in the name of farming. Lawmakers worked for only six months in their offices; yet, they were paid huge yearly allowances. The so-called agricultural break still obtains, only that it has now been reduced to three months.

The 1989 war disintegrated Liberia in the name of a "glorious revolution" by so-called Freedom Fighters under the eyes of law makers who could either call for a truce, the president's removal or resignation to save the state from more bloodbaths. The civil conflict divided the country into two unequal parts – "Monrovia, Liberia" under several interim regimes, and "Greater Liberia" under Mr Charles Taylor. The country's socio-political and economic fabrics crumbled. The Constitution was dethroned, leaving the state in the hands of series of transitional governments. These transitional governments ruled Liberia up to the election of Charles Taylor on July 19, 1997 and his subsequent installation in August the same year.

It was expected that good governance and the balance of power amongst the branches of government would prevail after the civil war. However, the Special Elections conducted under the Proportional Representative (PR) system created an imbalance in the legislature by giving the Ruling National Patriotic Party (NPP) absolute majority in the national legislature. The NPP selected over 90% of the Legislature. This was another model of Samuel Doe's 50th Legislature that was dominated by the ruling NDPL. The 51st Legislature was again subservient to the Executive. It passed national budgets disregarding the interest of constituencies. After the passage of the budgets, civil servants were not frequently paid. Lawmakers themselves were in some instances denied their benefits and salaries; yet, they passed subsequent budgets. They did not ratify concessions agreements in line with the laws. The Executive amassed enormous wealth from these illegal concessions like the Oriental Timber Company (OTC). Speaker Nyondweh Monkormana was retained after he was found guilty of perjury, a crime under the constitution of Liberia. The 51st Senate forced its Senate Pro Tempore, Charles W. Brumskine, out of office. Unlike the 50th Legislature, the 51st Legislature accepted the resignation of President Taylor under international pressure. President Taylor relinquished power to his Vice President, Moses Blah, though he had completed his six years term without holding elections. The 51st Legislature's resolution to accept transfer of power from Mr. Taylor to Blah was a good step in the right direction as it saved the country more blood bath.

The 52nd Legislature has some distinguishing characteristics from all others. It had the highest number of female lawmakers 14% (UNSG Report, 2007). It also had a good number of ex-combatants who actively participated in the Liberian Civil War. Some of the lawmakers were on international sanctions for their role in the civil war and close affinity with Charles Taylor.

Additionally, it was the first Liberian Legislature that was not initially dominated by members of the ruling Unity Party; however, due to political migration from opposition parties to the ruling party, most of the opposition lawmakers joined the ruling Unity Party. Initially, out of 64 Representatives, the ruling party had five, and out of 30 Senators it had ten; but. over time most of the legislators shifted from their parties to the ruling Unity Party. Despite the realignment in the Legislature, that First Branch of government was challenged in several ways. For instance, the 52nd Legislature admitted that it had serious limitations. It claimed that:

> The Legislature of Liberia lacked the institutional and trained manpower capacity to effectively perform the three primary functions of any legislative or parliamentary body: (1) representation; (2) law-making; and (3) oversight. To be effective, all critical components of the institution-the elected lawmakers, the staff (both direct and central), the work environment (offices, working tools and equipment, supplies), the mechanism for information gathering, processing, and articulation; and the framework for constituency contact and consultation – must be fully functional.

(Liberian Legislature Strategic Development Plan 2008-2012)

Regarding representation, there were no mechanisms or framework at the constituency level with time lines to ensure legislative consultation or reporting; although the Standing Rules of both Chambers of the Legislature designate Fridays of each week as "constituency day" and the statutes provide for legislative recess twice in a year – two weeks in April for the Easter Break, and six months (currently three months) as annual "Agriculture" break, there were no mechanisms or framework for the lawmakers to have regular contact with their constituencies. Equally, the Legislature did not have standard and regular reporting tools (journals, voting records, etc.) as information instruments for the constituencies. It was difficult to link the position of any one lawmaker to decisions of the Legislature and, therefore, hold any of them accountable at the constituency level.

On the lawmaking front, it is never a good practice to make laws without collecting and analyzing reference material and opinion about the law. Quality lawmaking is based on informed knowledge of the issues to be addressed. At the time, the legislative research and legal drafting capacity was and is still extremely weak. Not only were the staff deficient in this area, the institutional facilities were and are still lacking. The legislative archive has been in a complete state of disarray and disrepair. The legislative library was practically non-existent. There was neither system nor technical capacity to track bills as they move through the legislative processes. Sometimes, proposed bills stayed in committee room over a year. There were serious problems maintaining and circulating the legislative journal (the official record of deliberations of the institution).

Also, there was no mechanism for verbatim reporting. Many of the new lawmakers were not sufficiently versed on basic parliamentary rules, procedures and protocols governing the conduct of debate. Attitudes and perceptions of debating courtesies were not well refined. There were serious difficulties preparing for debates. Most of the time, lawmakers made oral presentations on the floor because of lack of capacity to prepared a priori and argue from written presentations that could be shared with constituents and the media. Often, the lawmakers reverted to motions that prematurely terminated debates when all the critical issues had not been fully and sufficiently articulated and exhausted. The lawmakers did not have the facilities or the technical expertise to transcribe and publish testimonies and results of public hearings on the internet, in local dailies, et al.

For its oversight role, the institutional organs through which lawmakers could conduct effective oversight were the plenary and the committees, the plenary being the highest decision-making body, while the committees served as technical arms. The Legislature did not have the state-of-the-art equipment needed to either record or transcribe proceedings; there were no recording and sound systems in the plenary and committee hearing rooms, or if there were, they were inadequate and inefficient. Stenographic machines and trained operators were non-existent. It was virtually impossible for the 52nd Legislature to maintain contact with both its local and international partners considering the new technological age. There was also no document reproduction capacity, nor public email and internet service facilities. There was no resource section from which one could access quality and well synthesized information.

The professional capacity of the staff was another great challenge. The poor staff capacity problem of the 52nd Legislature manifested itself in six primary ways: (1) excess personnel; (2) poorly trained; (3) poorly paid; (4) inadequately equipped; (5) absence of job description; and (6) highly politicized and patronized staffing arrangement. There was a dire need to rationalize and professionalize the strength of the legislative staff without jeopardizing the political standing of the lawmakers with their constituencies (Liberian Legislature Strategic Development Plan 2008-2012).

In addition to these challenges, the physical infrastructure of the Legislature, although rehabilitated by the Government of the United States, remains grossly inadequate to host all the working units of the institution. There is a grave need for additional offices. A legislative library is needed. Space is needed to restore the archives. Although some equipment has been provided for the resource centers of both Houses, the working space is extremely inadequate and not conducive for the purpose intended. There is less space for the clerical staff of the central administration of the Senate and House; no spacious office space for the personnel services departments; no adequate space for the legislative budget office, protocol and security; no visitor waiting area, et al. In the absence of these critical facilities, lawmakers and their staff are experiencing serious difficulties in carrying out their duties. Another area of critical infrastructural need is at the constituency level. At present, most lawmakers do not have home/constituency offices – buildings from which they could engage and dialogue with those they represent. Additionally, there are no communication facilities, besides mobile phones. Once the lawmakers are in Monrovia, they are cut off from their constituencies.

Despite these challenges, given the initial chemistry of the 52nd Legislature, hopes were that it would help create checks and balances in the Liberian political system. Unfortunately, it turned out to be another stooge of the Executive. Its Second Session was convened outside of Monrovia in violation of Article 40 of the Constitution. Despite Supreme Court ruling mandating the House of Representatives to return to "Status Quo Ante", the Head of State ignored that ruling and delivered her annual message at the illegal location. The House of Representatives illegally removed its Speaker after each of its members allegedly received $5000.00 USD bribe from the Executive.

The House also violated Article 49 of the Constitution by electing a new Speaker. This article calls for the election of a Speaker once every six years. The Senate suspended, for six months, its President Pro-Tempore for administrative ineptitude, later removed him and elected a new one, thereby equally violating Article 49 of the Constitution. Both the Senate and House of Representatives failed to exert their role in restructuring the Armed Forces of Liberia (AFL). The AFL was commanded by a foreign Chief of Staff, though there were qualified Liberians to occupy such post. The National Police, AFL and other security apparatuses were dissolved in violation of the CPA calling for restructuring of the security sector.

The 52nd Legislature refused to carry out civil service reforms at the Capitol Building. Support staff working at the Capitol remained at the mercy of their bosses, yet these staff were paid from the taxes of the people. At the time of this writing, legislative staff are still considered personal staff and therefore are not counted as civil servants. Only staff in Central Administration are considered civil servants. The Legislature held "Secret Sessions" otherwise known as Executive Sessions. Passage of budgets, ratification of concession agreements, and conclusion of more financially strategic decisions in the Legislature were reached at such sessions. This practice denied the public basic information on key decisions taken by their legislators and undermined transparency. Most of the confirmations done by the Senate were allegedly paid for by either the nominees or the Executive. Some confirmations were done behind closed doors by committees.

More besides, Legislative Committees were weak in carrying out their functions because they lacked the expertise. As earlier stated, most of the opposition representatives migrated to the ruling Unity Party. This brought into question the credibility and commitment of such legislators. They had used political institutions to ascend to power, but later deserted those very political institutions to join the ruling party. Some analysts explained this political mass migration as a function of the failure of such legislators to deliver on promises they made. As a result of failed promises, they risked re-election by their former parties; hoping that an eventual re-election of the status quo could lead to their appointments by the government.

The Senate for its part was accused of accepting bribes from the Executive to confirm confidants of the President. Such allegations need to be investigated and findings made public. The Senate should ensure that those confirmed are in the best interest of the State. Bribes for confirmation of nominees to executive positions should be abolished. On the budget front, the Legislature passed the proposed budget from the Executive without rigorously ensuring that budget lines captured actual development needs of the people in the villages, towns, districts and counties. In view of these and many more, the 53rd Legislature is no different from the 52nd, except that the 53rd has higher number of opposition politicians. Despite its opposition dominance, it dances to the tune of the Executive. The "4G passage" of Oil Block 13 whose signing fees to the entire government amounted to 50 million USD, the amendment of the Central Bank Act to prevent the Governor and his deputies from contesting the Liberian Presidency on grounds that Governor Mills Jones used the Bank's resources on micro finance programmes to gain popularity, thus paving the way for his possible contest and victory in 2017 Presidential and General Elections, and the March 2014 attempt by the Senate to increase registration fees of future legislative candidates from $750 USD to $7000 USD for Senators, and from $500 USD to $5000 USD for Representatives are topical flawed actions by the current lawmakers. The increment of registration fees for would-be legislative candidates caught the attention of this writer who posted the following on his blog:

The Liberian Senate is in Error to Introduce Amendment in the Elections Law Increasing Registration Fees for Legislative Candidates:

Illiteracy, greed and ignorance are few of the chronic diseases affecting our country, Liberia. Many people normally agree with decisions of public servants (legislature, executive appointees, judicial workers, civil servants, et al.) because they do not quite understand the implications or legal vicissitudes of actions taken by these people every moment in our national history.

One simple issue that has drawn my attention is the move by the Liberian Senate to amend the Elections Law of Liberia by increasing the fees to be paid by would-be contestants for Representative and Senate seats in future elections. Without going deep into the merits and demerits of this diabolical and unconstitutional law (something I would venture in sooner than later), I thought to first showcase a simple, but important constitutional clause that the Senate has bridged either knowingly or unknowingly.

In Article 34, the Legislature, amongst others, shall have the power:

d): to levy taxes, duties, imports, excise and other revenues, to borrow money, issue currency, mint coins, and to make appropriations for the fiscal governance of the Republic, subject to the following qualifications:

(i): all revenue bills, whether subsidies, charges, imports, duties or taxes, and other financial bills, shall originate in the House of Representatives, but the Senate may propose or concur with amendments as on other bills. No other financial charge shall be established, fixed, laid or levied on any individual, community or locality under any pretext whatsoever except by the expressed consent of the individual, community or locality. In all such cases, a true and correct account of funds collected shall be made to the community or locality, et al.

If the above must be the final word from our constitution, the organic laws of the State, one can safely assume that the fees levied on would-be legislative contenders would fall in the category of charges, if not taxes or duties. And as clearly indicated in (i), 'all revenue bills, whether subsidies, charges, etc. shall originate in the House of Representatives'..., "but the Senate may propose or concur with amendments on other bills". Unfortunately, the proposed amendment in the elections law incorporating increment in charges of fees on legislative candidates originates with the Senate, thus amounting to a constitutional bridge (if this part is a new law at all), or if one may argue that they have the right to propose amendment in line with the Constitution, then "No other financial charge shall be established, fixed, laid or levied on any individual, community or locality under any pretext whatsoever except by the expressed consent of the individual, community or locality", and in this case the individual, community or locality is the people of Liberia represented by the House of Representatives under the Representative Democratic system.

So, the question now is: will the Representatives concur with the Senate's ill-conceived bill or defend the interest of the poor people against whose interest the Senate has issued such amendment? Who is advising the Senate? Do they have legal advisers or political advisers? What is the House of Representatives saying? How can such a bill be proposed when the current poverty rate in Liberia is 74.6% in rural areas, 47.7% in urban sectors and 61.5% average at the national level (LISGIS 2008)? Should we not assume that this action is a demonstration of the fact that these lawmakers want to keep Liberians poorer in the interest of their selfish benefits? Can our people read the signs on the board or will they be blinded by party loyalty, ethnicity, et al.?

The House of Representatives has got a chance to redeem the image of the Legislature in this instance, though doubts abound that they will not concur based on previous bogus passages of criminal laws against the people of Liberia. Can they ratify a law that from its start contravenes the constitution, especially Article 30: indicating that "Citizens of Liberia who meet the following qualifications are eligible to become members of the Legislature:

a) for the Senate, have attained the age of 30 years and for the House of Representatives, have attained the age of 25 years;

b) be domiciled in the country or constituency to be represented not less than one year prior to the time of the election and be a taxpayer".

Let us wait and see, but my best bet is that we have a group of ignorant lawmakers who do not care about the spirit and intent of the Organic Laws of the Republic of Liberia, least to *talk about the interest of the people of Liberia. Alternatively, they have been obsessed by power and would do anything to deny the poor, and hardworking citizens (teachers, advocates, students, market women, farmers, community workers, etc.) the right to compete in national elections against them (current legislators). It would not be a surprise that should this amendment succeed, tomorrow could bring another amendment putting the fees at 100 thousand USD or more beyond the current proposal of increasing from $750 USD to $7000 for the Senate, and from $500 USD to $5000 USD for Representatives. And in such situation, those with the deepest pockets will contest and win, and keep the poor poorer while the rich would get richer. Liberians have your say; else, it may get too late. Just thinking aloud! (http://tomkaydor.blogspot. com.au/ 2014)*

Puzzled by the conduct of the 53rd Legislature, Charles Lawrence (2013) wrote on his blog under the caption "The Math behind the Numbers" as follows:

'When Cash and Promises Soar: Liberia's bi-cameral legislature comprises of 73 members of the lower house, called the House of Representatives and 30 members of the upper house, called the Senate. In 2014, Liberians will go to the polls to elect 15 of the 30 Senators for a tenure of nine years. These mid-term elections are a constitutional requirement that ensures that all the Senate seats are not vacant at the same time. In this piece, I argue that elections should be a growth industry where best ideas and character flourish above cash and false promises.

That post-war Liberia is a poor country is a fact undisputed by the evidence on the ground subject to the various data and statistics. In Sachs' assessment of poverty, it is when 'the margin of survival is extraordinarily narrow; sometimes it closes entirely' and common activities such as attending school becomes a 'hit-and-miss affair'. Poverty in its extreme means 'households cannot meet basic needs for survival, they are chronically hungry, unable to access health care, lack the amenities of safe drinking water and sanitation, cannot afford education for some or all of the children, and perhaps lack rudimentary shelter[i]' (Sachs, 2005; page 20).

There are many Liberians in their daily lives that will relate to the above situation and more. It is the need for change in the above situation that makes the elections process such a high stake for too many.

In such situation where large portion of the population exist in extreme poverty, the demands on elected representatives to meet basic needs such as school fees, meals, basic accommodation, and medical bills grow. The cost for elections also grows. Those contesting positions must demonstrate prior to being elected that they can meet these costs. As such, elections become a growth industry for the wrong reasons, an industry where cash not ideas flourish. situation is not helped by the prevailing notion, sustained through practice feeding on very absent civic education that legislators should solve day-to-day problems of members of their constituencies.

Sitting Senator Nyonblee Karnga-Lawrence of Grand Bassa County addressing the Senate of Pennsylvania in the United States of America concurred with this prevailing view 'because of poverty, the lack of education and the absence of good governance over a protracted period, the perceived responsibilities of a legislator have shifted to feeding the hungry, providing scholarships, building schools, building markets, building roads, youth empowerment programs, macro-credit for petty traders and market women; all of these are done by lawmakers from their personal resources[ii].' (Frontpage Africa, 10 December 2013)

Personal resources these elected representatives do have. The elected representatives have the tendency to reward themselves with handsome benefit package in salaries, allowances and expenses.

In the absence of a functioning welfare system that provides systematic and institutionalized support to people in need – housing, meals, school fees etc. A de facto welfare system pervades. One managed without accountability by individuals using political power and public resources to dish out cash, jobs and loans in exchange for future votes - votes which in such system can only bring the individuals closer to the economic resources.

Promises unfulfilled abound, since they are easier to make. Unfulfilled promises turned into lies. These lies do not morph into truths because they are told repeatedly. The truth remains that lies repeated simply erode people's trust in the political system.

In the absence of a healthy debate that scrutinizes the ideas and character of those wanting to represent the people, it is obvious that the notion of election is distorted. The focus must therefore be on the electors. It is support to the electors to better understand the implications of their votes, the use of their votes, how to make their votes translate into better outcomes. Voters have obligations to themselves and to future generations. For how long would they sacrifice the future in exchange of hand-outs to meet day to day needs?

Collier poignantly notes that 'change in the societies at the very bottom, must come from within.' In all these societies there are 'struggles between brave people wanting change[iii]' and vested interests opposing it. Each Liberian must sacrifice something, to be counted as part of the brave people wanting change. This can be manifested when one votes or chooses not to vote, when one gives, receives bribe or chooses not to, when one appoints friends, relatives into public offices or chooses not to, when one chooses not to assign public resources into personal use. It is the implication to others and the future generation that must underpin these decisions.

An army of the brave struggling for change can truly triumph over the few vested interests opposing such change. Each must distinguish him or herself, not on the basis of what he or she takes, but how much he or she gives in his or her examples and services, to contribute to a functional society, where institutions fulfil their mandates and are held accountable for doing so; where roads lead to markets, to towns, to villages to neighborhoods; where clean water flows into homes, schools, communities; where education harnesses the creativity and inventiveness of every child and youth.' (Italics mine)

In view of the foregoing, one can assume that the Legislature is far from being effective; lawmakers are self-interested and consider their constituents as a burden; yet, they continue to ignore the formulation of policies and laws that could transform the lives of the impoverished electorates who catapult them to power.

4.4 The Executive (1985-Present)

The Second Republic experienced what I call the "Dark Age" in the history of Liberia. In 1980, the first constitution of the Republic of Liberia was aborted by a military junta. This military group named and styled the People's Redemption Council ruled the country, and later transformed itself into civilian-like form but did not relinquish arms up to the adoption of the country's new constitution in 1985. As earlier stated, the presidential and general elections in 1985 were allegedly rigged thus laying the basis for political discontentment.

President Samuel Kanyon Doe engendered socio-political and economic reforms. He introduced the first graduate school in the country, granted scholarship to students of Agriculture and Forestry as well as Education, and constructed public buildings intended to relocate government ministries from privately-owned buildings. He began the construction of major highways and introduced a new currency (Liberian Dollar coins). The Green Revolution meant to make Liberia self-sufficient in food as well as other new progressive plans took root. However, there were still widespread abuses of the rights of citizens and suppression of political oppositions.

Despite these improvements, the dethroned True Whig Party regime fought systematically to undermine the peace and progress. A war of revenge was started by Charles Taylor and allies. The destruction and deaths caused by the war are self-evident. At the end of the first round of civil war that lasted for seven years, Charles Taylor was elected. Taylor won the lections overwhelmingly due to several factors, but prominent amongst them was fear that had he not won, he would have restarted another round of war.

This second regime in the Second Republic betrayed the confidence of the people. Taylor expelled peacekeepers and sidelined the Armed Forces of Liberia. He set up an elite Anti-Terrorist Unit (ATU), introduced the Special Operations Division (SOD) in the Liberia National Police (LNP) and organized former ex-combatants into the militia group. These various armed groups were only loyal to Taylor and his cronies, brutalized peaceful civilians, opposition politicians and even cracked down on foreign residents.

History is replete with the tyrannical actions of Taylor. However, he produced a new Liberian dollar currency (notes of 5, 10, 20, 50 and 100) which is currently being used alongside the United States Dollars. His bad governance practices, abuse of human and peoples' rights as well as non-cooperative stance with the international community landed him into the second round of civil war fought amongst the Liberia United for Reconciliation and Democracy (LURD), the Movement for Democracy in Liberia (MODEL) and those loyal to the government. Amidst intensity of the war, Taylor was charged with war crimes and crimes against humanity for his alleged involvement in the atrocities committed in Freetown. Taylor relinquished power to his Vice, Moses Z. Blah, owing to foreign interventions and was exiled in

Nigeria, where he was later repatriated from by the Ellen Johnson Sirleaf led government and arrested at the Roberts International Airport for trial at the Special Court in Freetown. Taylor was transferred to The Hague from Freetown due to fears of his trial stirring up tensions in the sub-region. He is currently serving a 50-year jail sentence in Britain.

Mr. Moses Blah became the second indigenous to serve as president of the Republic of Liberia. However, his tenure was very short. His few weeks regime achieved nothing much but allowed a transition to the National Transitional Government of Liberia formed in Ghana based on a peace deal brokered by the International Contact Group on Liberia (ICGL). He is credited for ushering in this transitional government and restoring Liberia's diplomatic relations with the People's Republic of China. As earlier mentioned, transitional regimes are not discussed herein because they were all unconstitutional regimes set up to exit the country from intermittent violent clashes.

The current regime is the fourth in the Second Republic. Ellen Johnson Sirleaf was elected amidst a controversial election in which the opposition Congress for Democratic Change (CDC) alarmed that it was denied victory. Fingers were pointed at the international community for favoring Madam Johnson-Sirleaf. Tensions arose, but the leader of CDC, George Weah, backed down. It is unclear as to whether the elections were free, fair, transparent and credible. However, the international community declared them free, fair, transparent and credible. The current government has high level of international support not only because Madam Ellen Sirleaf is the first Female African president, but also due to the fact that the international community, especially the ECOWAS, AU and United Nations, protects the fragile peace and stability as one of its peacemaking and peace building gains. To preserve regional and perhaps global peace, Liberia's progress out of a devastating war remains paramount as an international agenda.

The current Executive still dominates the other two branches of government in Liberia due to the lackadaisical attitude of the Legislature. This assertion can be clarified further based on the results of a sample survey this writer conducted in 2008 as part of his graduate thesis research. Synopsis of the survey are found in Chapter Five. Despite this domineering role of the Executive, some progress has been made in furtherance of democratic governance. For instance, the Executive proposed several reform frameworks that tend to increase accountability in the future if not now. The creation of the Anti-Corruption Commission, formulation and subsequent submission of a Code of Conduct for public officials to the National Legislature for ratification, the separation of the Revenue Department from the Ministry of Finance, the Creation of the General Auditing Commission wherein it operates under the aegis of the National Legislature as opposed to the Executive, et al. are all indicative of the progress being made to reduce corruption and increase national savings for investment in development and poverty reduction programmes. Although the National Legislature was instrumental in enacting these various anti-graft institutions into law, their incapacity and inability to have conceived such reforms brings their reputation and integrity into question.

Additionally, the Executive, in partnership with the International Community, has formulated several development programmes intended to transition Liberia from a war-ravaged state to a developmental one. Notably, the Executive has completed the implementation of the Poverty Reduction Strategy I and II. It has formulated the Agenda for Transformation and the "Liberia Rising Vision 2030". All these reform programmes have been aligned with the global agenda for the achievement of the Millennium Development Goals. Despite the necessities for these development programmes, the Legislature and the Judiciary hardly participated in the formulation and conclusion of these programmes. The Legislature, for instance, refused to attend the ceremony marking the official launch of the "Liberia Rising Vision 2030" in Gbarnga, Bong County.

Furthermore, all the regimes in the Second Republic have been offspring of crisis. The past ones did not uphold checks and balances. The present still does not. The current Executive removed Judge Milton Taylor for rendering judgment against the state; said case was retried and ruling upheld by a superior court. There have been widespread accusations against the Executive for inducing the Legislature to take unsolicited actions. The president delivered her annual message at the Organization of African Unity Conference Center deemed illegal by the Supreme Court in 2007 (Democrat, 2007). The full implementation of the Truth and Reconciliation Council (TRC) recommendations is yet another failure of the current regime. This, if not dealt with, could lead to another round of violence as crimes and abuse of human rights appear to be the source of power in Liberia.

Although there has been considerable progress under the current Executive, national reconciliation remains a fundamental challenge. National poverty rate still stands at 61.5%, corruption is rampant amongst the three branches of government, nepotism and favoritism are still on the rise. The failure of national government to curb these national vices also brings the Legislature's efficiency and effectiveness into question because they have got the constitutional duty to formulate policies and laws to combat such undemocratic tendencies, etc. The Legislature sits on several audit reports that could be used to arrest and prosecute public officials that have breached national trust. The Legislature itself has never been audited in the past ten years under the new democratic dispensation that Liberia now has.

4.5 The Judiciary (1985-Present)

In the Second Republic, the Judiciary is still very much the third branch of government. Its functions are more concerned with interpretation of law and the constitution and settling disputes mostly involving low social status individuals. Though there are several high-profile cases tried by the Judiciary, prosecuting lawyers lost most of them. For instance, the state lost the cases involving Mr Horatio Gould and Mr Dorley, former Director and Deputy Director, respectively of the National Social Security Corporation (NASSCOP), the corruption cases involving Edwin Snow, the Broplehs, et al. It also lost the widely publicized alleged coup plot case against Mr. Charles Julu, Mr. Andrew Dorbor and others. Further, the government abandoned the corruption case against former chairman Bryant and his cohorts.

The Judiciary today is largely made up of trained legal practitioners, yet it is not independent due to political interferences. By and large, the Judiciary collaborates with the Executive. For example, former Chief Justice Johnny Lewis, on request of the President, dismissed a Circuit Judge, James Zota. Judge Zota challenged this in the court of competent jurisdiction and was reinstated. The Judicial Branch of government was criticized by the Auditor General for withholding finances collected from levies, fines, etc. outside of government reporting and accounting systems. There are still delays in prosecution of cases. Several inmates languish in prisons without trial for offenses allegedly committed. There are still flaws in the justice and legal system of the country needing reform. The survey findings in Chapter Five also indicate the perception of some Liberians about the Judiciary.

CHAPTER V

SYNOPSIS OF A 2008 SURVEY OUTOMCES

In March 2008, this writer conducted a sample survey amongst students at the University of Liberia to gauge their perception about the application of the concept of checks and balances amongst the three branches of the Liberian Government. Out of a target sample of 150 students, only 100 students were able to complete and return their questionnaires. The selection of university students for the survey was based on two key assumptions. First, it was assumed that students at the University of Liberia have a good understanding of the concept of checks and balances and could better assess the implementation of said concept in their government. Second, it was assumed that university students represent the conscience of the society from various counties of the state; hence, their views could better serve as a representative sample of the views of the Liberian population in appraising the governance system of Liberia.

Question 1. Did you vote for a President, Senator and Representative in the 2005 elections?

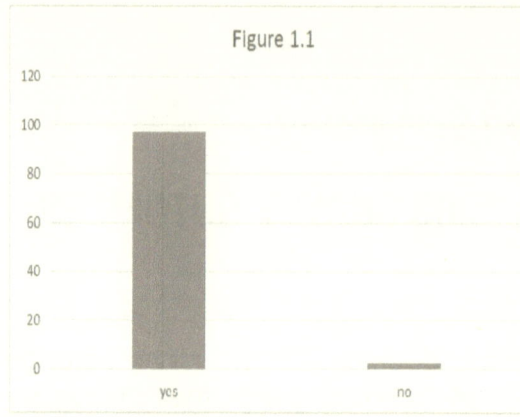

From Figure 1.1, 97% of the respondents participated in the 2005 Presidential and General elections and voted for presidential and legislative candidates. The other three percent did not.

Question 2. Having gone through 3 years of governance under this regime, grade the three branches of government on the following scale.

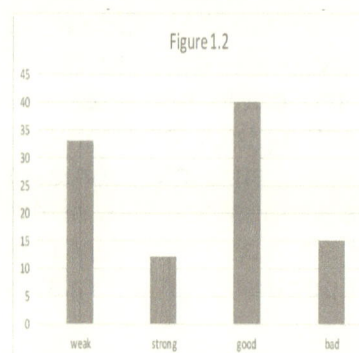

Based on this graph, the government in post conflict Liberia is largely viewed as a good government, though there was also high degree of skepticism about how strong the government is. About 15% of the interviewees saw the government as a bad government, whereas about 12% think it was a strong government.

Question 3. In your view, which branch of government is more powerful in Liberia presently?

In Figure 1.3, the respondents overwhelmingly believed that the Executive is the most powerful branch of government (rated at 90%), followed by the Legislature (about 6%) and the Judiciary (about 4%). This perception is indicative of the normal practice of Liberians to always call on the President to directly intervene in all national issues. The perception is a mismatch with the constitution which places the Legislature at the forefront of the people's representation. Although the President as Head of State and Government takes responsibility of what a government does, the Legislature shares similar responsibility because, as direct representatives of the people. their role is paramount to the progress of the Liberian society just as the US Congress is the epicenter of national and international decision making in the United States. They have got the responsibility to

Figrue 1.3

articulate and enshrine into law the people's whims and caprices; sadly, this is not the case in Liberia.

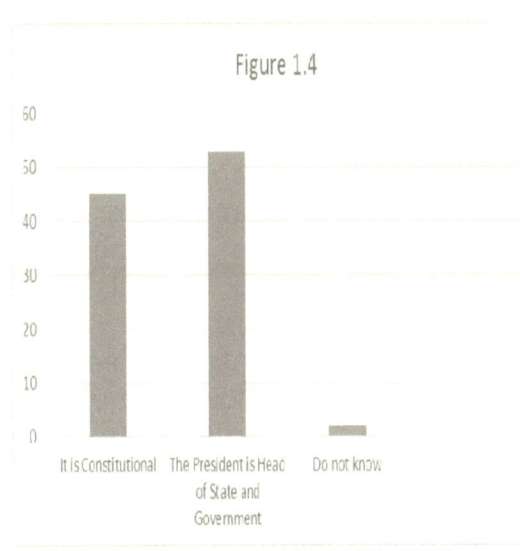

Figure 1.4

Question 4. If your answer is the Executive, why do you think so?

This follow-up question to question three was left opened for interviewees to comment. Amongst comments written, there were three concentrations. Many say that the

President is the Head of State and Government and therefore carries more power. Others thought that the domineering nature of the Executive stems from the Constitution, while a minute portion did not really have any view about this. The views expressed here seem to represent a cross section of the views of the Liberian populace. This can be deduced from various radio talk shows on which callers regularly refer to the President as the person responsible for every development issue and problem in the country. Callers hardly think the Legislature should be directly accountable to the people. More astonishing in this feedback is that university students who were assumed to be conscious of the constitutional provisions of checks and balances had a little understanding of what this concept means. This brings home the argument that Article ten (10) of the Constitution needs to be fulfilled if the people must know and understand their constitution. Articles ten (10) calls for the teaching of the Constitution in all institutions of learning in Liberia.

Question 5. If you think the Executive is powerful and the Legislature is weak, what are the factors responsible?

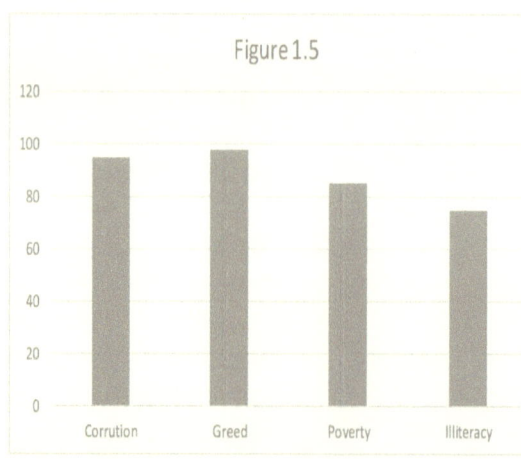

Figure 1.5

Answers to this question were quite thought provoking. Respondents graded greed as the major factor responsible for the weakness of the Legislature. Corruption was ranked second, followed by poverty and illiteracy. There were some interesting comments about the Legislature receiving bribes from the Executive to pass laws, confirm presidential nominees, and ratify concession agreements.

Some referred to "Brown Envelops" meaning lobby fees, etc., as the key motives for which lawmakers' campaign to get elected. The question though is that these very people are the voters who elected the legislators; yet cannot hold them accountable when they proceed along unethical lines and engage in practices that these respondents considered repugnant to the acceptable conduct of legislators.

Question 6. Select the best description amongst the following based on your perception of the Judiciary?

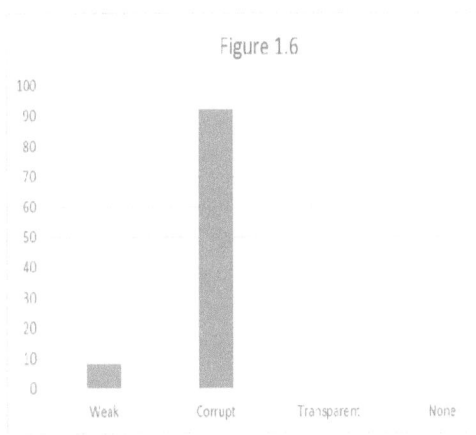

Figure 1.6

The Judiciary for its part was graded above 90% as being very corrupt. This ranking speaks to general feelings amongst poorer people that justice is for the rich. The Judiciary needs to make frantic efforts to reverse such perception by dispensing justice based on transparency, equity and fair play.

Question 9. Can the Legislature be strong?

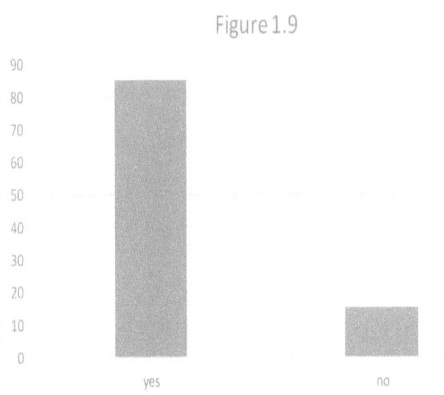

Figure 1.9

About 85% of the interviewees thought that the Legislature can become a strong branch of government, as opposed to 15% of the respondents who are pessimistic about the robust nature of the Legislature. This graph further supports findings under question three where the respondents saw the Executive as the most powerful branch of government in Liberia.

Question 10. If yes, how?

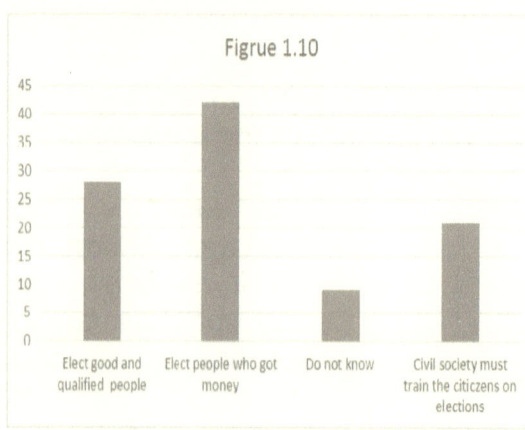

Figure 1.10 shows another fascinating result of the survey. Again, this question was left open for respondents to write out what they thought could be done to remedy the situation of corruption, poverty, greed and illiteracy which they ranked in response to question five in Figure 1.5. Interestingly, comments focused on how "people should elect good and qualified people, vote for those who have money, and the role civil society needs to play". It is quite unclear what it means when one talks about good and qualified people because this is normative and subjective. Who is good and qualified? At least there is a constitutional provision in Article 30, which says 'Citizens of Liberia who meet the following qualifications are eligible to become members of the Legislature.

a) for the Senate, have attained the age of 30 years and for the House of Representatives, have attained the age of 25 years;

b) be domiciled in the country or constituency to be represented not less than one year prior to the time of the election and be a taxpayer'.

Judging from the above, there is no requirement on academic qualification which most of the respondents thought as indicated in their written responses. Even if one where to attach qualification to legislative positions, how certain can one be by assuming that academically qualified persons can make good lawmakers? Although it is imperative to have educated and informed legislators in the contemporary technologically dynamic world, it would require an amendment in the constitution to place a limit on the level of education one must have to become a legislator. Similarly, how certain can it be that those with financial consequence can make "good" lawmakers? It could be possible to have a poor person becoming a legislator and keeping his or her integrity, and as well promoting pro-poor policies. However, the view of these respondents based on an analysis of the written comments point to the issue of lawmakers being greedy and corrupt during their service as legislators. Placing a tag on how much someone should own to become lawmaker may rob the poor of the opportunity to serve in such capacity.

Although the level of education and poverty are two controversial issues relative to qualifying for legislative positions, history shows that during the rule of President Tubman, the illiterate chiefs who became lawmakers had no idea on what legislative functions were about. It therefore goes without saying that lawmakers need to be competent, academically qualified and experienced individuals so that their education, experience, and competence can valuably help them become effective and efficient lawmakers representing the interests of their constituents. Additionally, in recent times, several lawmakers became legislators before going back to complete secondary school, or enter colleges and universities, thereby distracting them from the cumbersome function of lawmaking. They also used their political positions to compromise enrollment procedures at academic institutions-an act counterproductive to the integrity and independence of academic institutions. Some legislators are less qualified. compared to their legislative staff members. It would therefore be a good idea were educational qualification to be placed on legislative candidates.

On the question of poverty, there is a need to define what poverty is. In the African context, and for Liberia specifically, wealth is not only measured in dollars and cents. The riches of persons and individuals are measured in what property they own, the cattle they raise and own, how many children they have and the number of wives they keep and cater for, etc. These Afrocentric views of wealth may be equally controversial, but the measurement of wealth as a prerequisite for qualification to contest legislative seats should not be based on dollars and cents. It is possible that corrupt officials could use their ill-gotten wealth to become lawmakers for the very people they have kept poor through their corrupt and mischievous acts. However, it is also equally important that those becoming representatives and senators for the people must hold high moral grounds and reputation in their constituencies. As leaders normally become models for the youth, it is important to have individuals with an enviable track record of advocacy, people-centered history, development-oriented views and transformative agenda become qualified candidates for the Legislature. Above all, it is love for the people and country that forms the bedrock for "good lawmakers".

Lastly, there were comments about the role of the civil society training the citizens about how to vote and who to vote for. This is a fundamental concern, especially in a country whose electorates are predominantly illiterate. I quite agree that the civil society needs to create awareness amongst citizens on their rights and obligation, including the right to vote. The civil society, however, cannot be the decider of which candidate electorates must vote for. The electorates can be trained about how to vote, what constitutes good representation and the quality of good leadership. It would be left solely with them to determine their choices based on either party or the platform of the candidates in a particular electoral competition.

The National Elections Commission and the national government at large also have a greater role to the citizens in educating them about their rights and responsibilities under the constitution and laws of Liberia. One key issue that needs to be addressed by national government is the mass education of its citizens, which will allow people to become rational thinkers and decision makers. With mass literacy amongst the population, electoral candidates would not easily get votes through falsehood, undemocratic tendencies, and the use of stolen or borrowed campaign finances as is normally the case in Liberia. More importantly also is the fact that the National Legislature needs to enact laws that will ensure that mass education is supported by the government for the liberation of the people in the various constituencies.

CHAPTER VI

THE CURRENT GOVERNANCE SITUATION

6.1 The National Dimension

Liberia's 14-year civil war displaced about 800,000 Liberians, while an estimated 250,000 were killed. Thousands were sexually abused, harassed and a significant fabric of the society has greatly been undermined; destruction of the nation's infrastructure and economy is self-evident (UNDAF, 2007). The Comprehensive Peace Agreement (CPA) of August 2003 and United Nations Security Council Resolution (SCR) 1509 availed a new opportunity for peace and stability in Liberia. An international peacekeeping force was deployed to create landing ground for the National Transitional Government of Liberia (NTGL) formed in Ghana. Under the NTGL, the Results-Focused Transitional Framework (RFTF) was launched and about $700 million US disbursed - largely on elections, security, basic social services and humanitarian interventions (RFTF, 2005).

Some 103,000 ex-combatants, of whom an estimated 12,000 were children, were disarmed and demobilized under the internationally backed process of Disarmament, Demobilization, Rehabilitation and Reintegration (DDRR) in 2004. More than 700,000 of the internally displaced persons and refugees are back home, while some huge number remains in countries of asylum in the sub-region and other western countries (NCDDRR, 2004)

In late 2005, Ellen Johnson Sirleaf was elected as the first female president in Africa. Since then, the government and people of Liberia, with enormous goodwill and support from the international community, have achieved peace and stability; however, reconciliation remains a great challenge. The government has no clearly articulated agenda for genuine reconciliation, yet there is still widespread emphasis on the Unity Party led government achieving much rather than what Liberian, together, can achieve. The government clings to individual loyalty, sidelining the party, as opposed to meritocratic leadership anchored on national unity. There seem to be a reawakening of the oligarchy dethroned in 1980 by Samuel Doe and other enlisted men of the Armed Forces of Liberian.

Despite the above challenges, the government evolved and implemented an interim Poverty Reduction Strategy (iPRS) following a 150-day transitional Action Plan. The iPRS revised the civil service code and streamlined the procurement processes. Internal controls are being introduced, financial management procedures overhauled and there is a semblance of fighting corruption; yet corruption is still widespread as corrupt practices go unpunished. Normally government officials suspected of corruption are transferred from one government entity to another for administrative reasons or the suspicions totally ignored. Cases in point include the removal of executives of National Port Authority (NPA) and their reassignment, the retention of the Chair of the National Investment Commission (NIC) as well as some deputy ministers accused of signing over $150m contract on a tax freed basis in collaboration with the NIC boss in violation of the law, etc. Thus far, the Chief Executive has declared the contract null and void. Other cases in point have to do with the removal of Mr Harry Greaves from the Liberia Petroleum Corporation on corruption charges, without prosecution; the removal of one of the Deputy Ministers of Finance on corruption charges and her reassignment at the Ministry of Foreign Affairs and subsequently reassigned to Germany as Liberia Ambassador;

the removal of the Minster of Public Works, Lusinne Donzo, and the reassignment in the Office of the President as advisor on Public Works, etc.

All three branches of government have come under vehement criticism for corrupt acts that are not yet appropriately investigated and remedied. The Governance and Economic Management Assistance Program (GEMAP) has been implemented with strong support from Liberia's development partners amidst these corrupt allegations. The United Nations Security Council lifted sanctions on Liberia's diamonds and timber, though it remains unclear how these resources contribute to current development needs. The Legislature has a pivotal role to play by enacting laws to regulate investment policies regarding the natural resources of the country as well as provide for judicious allocation of resources for national development, especially focusing on neglected counties and communities.

Whilst there is much to celebrate, we all must recognize that Liberia is at a critical juncture. Continued support to the government by the people of Liberia is quintessential to ensure that the gains made to date are built upon for a true consolidation of the peace. The existing peace needs to account equitable, inclusive, and sustainable nationally owned development. To do this, there is a need for fiscal discipline, legal reforms, vibrant civil society, and rule of law. Here, the three branches of government need to strongly adopt checks and balances for the growth and development of the country and its young democracy.

The current government has made tremendous gains, though it still faces serious socio-political and economic issues begging genuine redress. Although with the support of the international community bilateral partners, the government endeavors to restore Liberia to its pre-war status, poverty is widespread and reconstruction efforts are challenged by the huge infrastructure deficit (United Nations in Liberia 2013) inherited from the civil war. The current poverty rate in Liberia is 74.6% in rural areas, 47.7% in urban sectors and 61.5% average at the national level (LISGIS 2008). The estimated cost of reviving Liberia's damaged transport and energy infrastructure to the pre-war status is about two and half billion US Dollars at a time the country's current national budget is a little over 500 million (Ministry of Finance 2013). Poor infrastructure therefore impedes economic growth, creates limited access to basic social services and as a result government's effort to reduce poverty is stagnated. My assumption is that if the country has good infrastructure (transport, electricity and water systems), Liberia will experience economic growth and development and poverty will be reduced.

Moteff et al (2004) define infrastructure as 'basic facilities, services, and installations needed for the functioning of a society'. This means that without good infrastructure, a given society will not function well. Based on this premise, I am of the view that due to poor infrastructure, Liberia cannot function as an effective state that can provide for the security and the wellbeing of its people in an efficient manner. Presently, major roads linking the rural parts of the country are in a deplorable state. The 51.3 percent of rural inhabitants in the country are gravely affected by the lack of basic social services. Additionally, due to the poor transport system, rural residents lack access to basic services, including schools, health and markets. For instance, health indicators show that while mortality rate in rural areas is 84 per every1000 births compared to urban areas where mortality stands at 68 per every 1000 births, maternal mortality is 994 per 100,000, and under age five mortality is 110 per 1000 births (LDHS 2007; UN One Programme 2013). Most of the maternal and under five mortality rates occur in the rural communities where efficient health facilities and personnel are scarce.

Just as the health sector, which is grossly affected by poor infrastructure, the education sector is equally affected by said condition. For example, the Ministry of Education (2009)

Education Sector Plan calls for compulsory nine-year basic education, comprising six years of free primary and three years of junior secondary education completion. Despite this progressive free and compulsory primary education policy, majority of rural residents and the urban poor cannot send their children to free schools because public schools are very limited, and the existing ones lack adequate facilities and trained teachers. Most schools in the country are operated by either religious institutions or private individuals whose basic objective is to amass profit through education due to the huge gap created in this sector by the scarcity of public schools. The current net enrolment in primary school stands at 34%, and grade six completion rate in the entire country is 35% (United Nations in Liberia 2013). These figures imply that about 65% of the children in the country are out of school. Amongst these are children who enroll in schools, but dropout due to lack of fees, tuition and other basic education materials required for regular school attendance.

The lack of adequate safe drinking water amongst the general population is another social problem facing the country. Access to piped water fell from 15 percent of the population in 1986 to less than 3 percent in 2008 (LISGIS 2008). Project Liberia (2013) indicates that ten years following the fratricidal and devastating civil war, 'one in four Liberians has access to safe drinking water'. Despite the low record of deliverables in the water and sanitation sector of Liberia's reconstruction process, there were some positive outcomes. There are differences on the magnitude of the improvement. The Ministry of Health and Social Welfare (MOHSW 2011, p. 6-7 citied in IMF 2012 Liberia Country Report) indicates that the share of households with access to clean water increased from 67 to 75 percent, 2007 to 2009, however wide disparities exist between urban and rural households.

Clean and safe drinking water is mostly obtained from hand pumps and bold holds. Access to sanitary toilet facilities rose from 39 percent to 50 percent nationwide, with improvement in rural as well as urban areas (CWIQ 2010, p.120-1 cited in IMF 2012 Country Report). Despite these improvements, the World Health Organization (WHO) Country Office in Liberia reported that half of all Liberians have no access to a toilet facility, hence defecating up streams or in open areas. It further added that outbreaks of water-borne diseases like cholera occur regularly, and that as many as one in five deaths in Liberia are blamed on water and sanitation problems.

While poor transport system hinders access to adequate and efficient education, health facilities and water, it also undermines economic recovery, growth and development in post conflict Liberia. The rural residents in the country live mostly on subsistence farming, though some produce cash crops for trade and commerce. They basically produce goods for consumption and trade their surplus to obtain necessities that are locally unavailable and can be obtained from urban markets. Due to the absence of farm to market roads, these rural farmers cannot transport goods and services from villages and towns to markets within the country. This does not only serve as a disincentive for unproductive rural households, but also increases hunger, disease and poverty amongst them. The urban poor for their part lives in slum communities where they are entrapped in poverty and disease. Currently, Liberians living under one US Dollar a day are about 63%, and the population living in extreme poverty stands at 47.9% (LISGIS 2007).

Liberia is amongst the 104 countries covered by the Multidimensional Poverty Index (MPI), where about 1.56 billion people are estimated to live in multidimensional poverty. The country is part of the countries with the highest percentages of 'MPI poor' with a rank of 84% chasing Ethiopia with 87%, and leading Mozambique and Sierra Leone at 79% and 77%, respectively (Human Development Index 2013). Despite this alarming poverty status, the HDI (2013) labels Liberia as one of fourteen countries that have recorded impressive HDI gains of more than 2 percent annually since 2000. These countries in order of improvement are Afghanistan, Sierra Leone, Ethiopia, Rwanda, Angola, Timor-Leste, Myanmar, Tanzania, Liberia, Burundi, Mali, Mozambique, Democratic Republic of the Congo, and Niger. Most of them are low-HDI African countries, with many, including Liberia, emerging from long periods of armed and civil conflicts.

In addition to the poor transport system which undermines adequate access to basic social service in Liberia thereby subtracting from efforts aimed at poverty reduction, the absence of adequate supply of electricity equally forestalls economic recovery, growth and recovery. Liberia has limited energy output. For instance, the pre-war 170-megawatt power generation capacity and national grid were destroyed during the civil war. A Little over 0.1 percent of households had access to electricity. Installed power generation capacity obtained from diesel generators is little more than 2 megawatts per million people. It costs $0.77 to generate one per kilowatt-hour, which is exceptionally high by any standard (Africa Infrastructure Country Diagnostic Report 2010). Power tariff of $0.43 per kilowatt-hour is about three times the average for Africa, which is already very high by global standards. The country's singular dam, the Mount Coffee Hydro Plant, rehabilitation cost is estimated at US$ 207 million. Due to the lack of resources, government has been unable to refurbish the dam since the cessation of the civil conflict for the past ten years. With the European Central Bank (ECB), Germany and Norway providing grants and soft loans of $65 million, $32 million and $75 million, respectively, as well as governments commitment of %45 million, reconstruction of the dam has begun and is set to be completed by Dec 2015 (Ministry of Finance 2014).

Poor transport and lack of access to basic social services combined undermine economic growth and development in Liberia. The country has attracted over 16 billion USD in foreign direct investment (Liberia National Investment Commission 2014). These investments are intended to restore

Liberia's economy to its pre-war status and set the stage for economic growth and development. They are also to increase employment directly by employing thousands of citizens, and indirectly by creating economic opportunities, thereby boosting private sector development and local investments amongst nationals and aliens. Unfortunately, due to poor transport and lack of electricity, majority of the concessionaires have yet to begin full scale operation to yield the needed resources and employment envisioned in the concession agreements. The BRE/Vattenfall Wood Ship Export and BR Power 35MW Power Plants investment projects, for example, have failed, and the concession closed deliberately partly due to falsehood and deceit on the part of the concession, and the government's inability to have done due diligence in signing the concession agreement. Concessions that are currently operational face enormous transaction cost due to lack of electricity, water and good roads. The matrix below indicates all concession agreements entered between government and foreign investors, excluding those signed with oil companies now exploring for commercial offshore oil quantities. Despite these agreements, the actual outcome of investments leaves much to desire.

Figure 1.1 Foreign Direct Investment in Liberia (Source: Liberia National Investment Commission)

SECTOR	CAPITAL	POTENTIAL JOBS	LOCATION
Mining			
Revised Mittal Steel Agreement	$1.6 Billion	3,000	Nimba Buchanan
China Union/Bong Mines MDA	$2.6 Billion	3,000	Bong
Seversta/Putu MDA	$2.0 Billion	2,000	Grand Gedeh
BHP Billiton/Kitoma, Goe Fentro MDA	$1.8 Billion	2,500	Lofa, Nimba
AmLib (Kokoya and Cestos)	$100 Million	200	Bong, Nimba, River Cess
Africa Aura (Gola Konneh)	$150 Million	200	Cape Mount
Agriculture			
ADA/LAP Commercial	$30 Million	200	Lofa
Decoris Oil Palm Plantation	$64 Million	1,000	Maryland
Cavalla Rubber Plantation Rehabilitation	$65 Million	1,000	Maryland
Sime Darby Gurthrie Plantation	$800 Million	30,000	Cape Mount
Golden Veroleum/ Southeast Plantations	$1.7 Billion	40,000	Maryland, Sinoe, Grand Kru
Equatorial Palm Oil	$100 Million	10,000	Grand Bassa
Hotels			
Robert L. Johnson/ Kendeja Hotel	$10 Million	160	Monsterrado

Golden Gate Hotel/ SKD Stadium	$8 Million	100	Monsterrado
Cape Hotel, Golden Key, Palm Springs, Royal	$50 Million	400	Monsterrado
Industries			
BRE/Vattenfall Wood Ship Export	$200 Million	700	Grand Bassa
BR Power 35MW Power Plants	$150 Million	300	Grand Bassa
CEMENCO New Mill	$20 Million	100	Montserrado
Forestry			
5 Timber Sale Contracts	$20 Million	500	Various Counties
4 Forest Management Contracts	$60 Million	2,000	Various Counties
Petroleum			
Anardako/Repsol/ Oranto/Africa Petroleum/European Hydrocarbon	$500 Million	200	—
20 New Total Stations	$20 Million	1,000	Various Counties
Finance			
Guarantee Trust Bank	$8 Million	100	Montserrado
Access Bank	$6 Million	100	Montserrado
UBA Bank	$8 Million	100	Montserrado
Lib. Enterprise Dev. Fund	$8 Million	10	Montserrado
Infrastructure			
APM Terminal, Port of Monrovia, Privatization	$100 Million	250	Montserrado

In view of the above, and based on government's vision to rebuild the country, grow its economy and ultimately reduce poverty, Liberia implemented Poverty Reduction Strategy (PRS) one and two between 2006 and 2012. The country aspires to become a middle-income country by the year 2030 (Liberia Rising Vision 2030 2013). The country that was on the cusp of becoming a middle-income country by the 1980s, and was one of the highest-income countries in Africa, though grew without development (Clower 1966), is presently one of 35 low-income countries (LICs) in the world, and one of 26 Sub-Saharan African countries. One key factor challenging this ambitious aspiration is the huge infrastructure deficit confronting the post-conflict state. But the question is how can the country overcome its current weak infrastructural challenge, restore social services, etc. when its national budget is far lower than these huge investment projects require? This is a fundamental question because the country's real GDP remains at $1233 USD, GDP per capital at $328 USD and the growth rate is 6.1 % (Ministry of Finance 2010). This growth rate considered by the World Bank, International Monetary Fund et al. as impressive, does not translate into conducive living for the people.

So, what can the government do to service its infrastructure deficit? Can it borrow loan, or can it attract donor support to undertake these projects? Alternatively, can the government pursue joint government-private sector partnership to fund these huge infrastructure projects? Amongst these three options, only two are feasible because the loan option has international limitations. Even though Liberia got a debt waiver of over four billion US Dollars from the International Monetary Fund and the World Bank (International Monetary Fund 2010), the World Bank and International Monetary Fund have placed a borrowing ceiling on the country.

In development, it seems, you cannot do anything until you can do everything. That is the idea behind the "big push" theory (Rosenstein-Rodan 1957). Outlined by Paul Rosenstein-Rodan in 1943, this theory states that even the simplest activity requires a network of other activities and that individual firms cannot organize such a large network; so, the state or some other giant agency must step in. therefore, it is impossible for the government alone, given its current economic and financial status, to restore the country's damaged infrastructure. Also, private investors cannot maximize the desired profits amidst the infrastructure challenge; but, at the time, they do not wish to risk their capital to undertake this task alone. That infrastructure and social services are considered public goods, private investors, driven by profits motives, consider investment in public facilities a government's responsibility. But can investors and concessionaires gain by conducting business in a hostile environment, thereby increasing transaction costs? Is it not ideal to collaborate with government in building the desired infrastructure such that both governments, the investors and the general public will utilize to boost trade, economic growth and development and reduce poverty?

In response to these questions, the 'Big Push' theory as presented by Rosenstein-Rodan (1957) seems the only viable methodology through which Liberia can maximize investment, grow its economy and reduce poverty. Based on this theory, a Big Push or a big and comprehensive investment package can be helpful to bring economic development". For this to occur, a certain minimum amount of resources must be devoted for developmental programmes, if the success of programmes is required. As some ground speed is required for the aircraft to airborne, certain critical amount of resources need to be allocated for development activities, in the case of Liberia, a combination of investment in the social capitol from the government, private investors and donors is required to invest in infrastructure consisting of the means of transportation, communication and energy resources. As no piecemeal allocation in economy can move on the path of economic development, investment in social overhead capitol is something necessary for economic development. With economic growth and development, government can allocate more resources to basic social services, and reduce poverty. The government needs to therefore attract donors' support while engaging in joint government-private sector partnership to address the infrastructure challenge and restore basic social services.

The three branches of government, especially the Legislature, must take the lead. The Agenda for Transformation must be supported through resource allocation in the national budget by the national Legislature. The Executive must be more transparent and accountable to woo donor and international support to government policies; and the state must promote bottom-up approach development planning and implementation. Undoubtedly, with out checks and balances amongst the branches of government, much can not be achieved as one branch could dominate and sway development and recovery strategies in either wrong or right directions, as has been in the past, or undermine the zest for good governance in post-war Liberia. The Legislature is the direct representation of the people. Therefore, it must be effective, efficient and diligent in doing its work. The people depend on the Legislature for their needs to be met. They (legislators) should henceforth endeavor to working in the best interest of the state, not for their personal gains and incentives.

6.2 The International Dimension

The international community has so far endeavored to treat the government of Liberia as a unit with three parts. It does not deal with the government in a fragmented manner. For instance, the United Nations Development Assistance Framework (UNDAF) sets out the specific areas of response of the United Nations to Liberia's poverty reduction and development challenges. The UN holistically responds to the needs of the three branches as well as the citizens in general. Informed by the analysis of the United Nations Common Country Assessment for Liberia conducted in 2006, five UNDAF outcomes were articulated, corresponding to the timeframe of the PRS and even moving beyond. These outcomes were further validated through a process of regional consultations involving county and district authorities and reflect national priorities. Given that the United Nations intends to remain responsive to national needs, its past and present UNDAF and associated programmes are being evolving processes that can be modified as the Government's strategy develops, and new data become available. The Executive, Legislature, Judiciary and the local communities should therefore participate in all development processes to be well positioned to take on where the UN support would wane.

All branches of government have a role to play in realizing the outcome of the UNDAF that include, but not limited to, increasing capacity of national and local authorities to provide security, manage conflict and prevent violence while respecting human rights. National economic policies and programmes are to be implemented to support equitable, inclusive and sustainable socio-economic development. Related United Nations agency country programmes help ensure that national management and implementation frameworks are strengthened along with capacities for Millennium Development Goals (MDG)-oriented policy planning, analysis and monitoring. Increased access to decent and productive employment and sustainable livelihood opportunities is essential, especially for vulnerable groups. A comprehensive effort to improve household food security is being undertaken with sustainable natural resource management, environmental protection and the promotion of gender equality. All these lofty ideal responses to national priority cannot achieve the desired benefits if the three branches of government do not deliver on their constitutional mandates.

Moreover, the rule of law, democratic, accountable and transparent governance is to be advanced in a participatory and inclusive manner and in accordance with human rights standards. Associated country programme outcomes attempt to promote and sustain rights-based justice and the delivery of services and the strengthened representation - especially for women. National, regional and local mechanisms are being enhanced to uphold human rights and provide social protection. The UN used the County Support Team (CST) approach to bolster the capacity of local authorities in the 15 counties of Liberia. All Counties have administrative buildings constructed and or furnished under this programme. This is in direct support of decentralization of governance. The United Nations also supports the legislative and electoral systems, partnering with civil society organizations. The Legislature needs to advance these efforts by enacting relevant laws to foster economic growth and development and promote democratic culture ultimately.

Improved health and education, with an emphasis on reduced maternal and child mortality and increased learning achievement, are another element of response by the international community to national priorities. This response guides the United Nations support for basic social services in Liberia. Results are being achieved through increased access to quality education and reduced maternal and under-five mortality. Specific nutrition, water, sanitation and hygiene awareness outputs are being addressed and advanced daily. Notwithstanding, the government still does not allocate enough resources for hospitals, clinics and schools. More money is allotted to benefits and salaries for government officials. The Legislature is obliged to ensure that national budget includes substantive budgetary allotments to fund these initiatives.

Amongst Liberia's many challenges is the issue of HIV and AIDS that has deadly consequences. The United Nations and other partners make commitment to work collectively in this area by providing support to the creation of an enabling environment and capacities to prevent the spread of HIV and AIDS. The United Nations also engages with partners to provide treatment, care and support to people living with this deadly disease, and to address its related stigma and discrimination. However, the nation's budget lacks substantive allocation, if any, for this time bomb that could ruin the productive fabric of the state. Lack of economic opportunities is one of the factors forcing young girls and boys to engage in prostitution, thus opening even wider chances for the deadly virus to spread.

Deeply rooted domestic violence and sexual-and-gender-based violence necessitate the promotion of equality and the mainstreaming of gender issues into national policies. This is tied into the formulation of transformative policies and enactment, and implementation of non-discriminatory laws, a responsibility, to a larger extent, of the National Legislature. The United Nations took practical steps in the past by hiring a Coordinator for the prevention of sexual exploitation and abuse to raise awareness and put the necessary mechanisms in place to reduce, if not to get rid of, this social menace. It is yet unclear as to whether the government has such instruments in place to deter SEA in workplaces. Some analysts strongly believe that most government officials hire their love ones as secretaries, etc. in their offices. This act must be reversed.

On the other hand, for Liberia to move successfully towards achieving MDGs and securing human rights for all its citizens, a fundamental recognition and commitment to avert further conflict is paramount. Policies and programmes must address the root causes of conflict in Liberia and work towards sustaining the peace. This requires a robust causal, role pattern, capacity and gap analysis. The international community is making every effort to ensure that its initiatives serve to reduce, rather than increase, inequalities and inequities. The reduction of poverty will depend on the inclusion of youth in the economic and political life of the country.

Again, the National Legislature needs to formulate pro-poor policies to address widespread inequality in Liberia. In the same vein, capacity development is central to rebuilding a fragile state. The United Nations strives to support the Government to realize its commitments to the people of Liberia by supporting the establishment of effective institutions and systems, identifying capacity gaps and providing technical support for a functioning civil service. The United Nations and other partners aligned their responses towards common objectives, achieving outcomes that drew on the comparative advantage of individual institutions to help ensure that the Government can realize the principles and goals of the Millennium Declaration for all Liberians (UNDAF, 2007). Can the National Legislature enact laws that will address the capacity gap in Liberia, or will the state continue to utilize the skills of consultants with huge allowances to rebuild the country?

The Government of Liberia through an education law could bridge the capacity gap in four years. It could adopt a "Liberian styled Higher Education Contribution Scheme", modeled after the Australian government's Higher Education Contribution Scheme introduced in 1989 and is now being practiced by other countries, including South Africa, Chile, Thailand and Britain (Gans et al. 2012). Under this scheme, the Australian government and those countries now practicing similar policy give loan to its citizens to attend colleges or universities. Upon graduation, the students begin to work and repay government the money spent on their education. This process leaves no one behind, except those who refuse to enroll into colleges and universities. Could the Government of Liberia, through the Legislature, allocate resources to jump start similar noble initiative to allow those disadvantaged Liberians wishing to gain high education benefit? Such interventions are the sort of pro-poor policies that our National Legislature needs to pursue for the development and transformation of Liberia.

On the budgetary front, the Legislature must ensure that national budgets passed reflect and align with priority areas being supported by international partners. Better still, the Government can ensure that the international community target resources to priority areas deemed expedient for poverty alleviation and national development. As such, donor monies would be focused on a set of national priorities that national budget cannot adequately support. The Executive, for its part, has to ensure that resources allocated are judiciously spent and accounted for, while the Judiciary has an enormous role to play in ensuring that the rule of law prevails to provide for a peaceful environment through which economic growth and development can obtain. Without justice and the rule of law, peace and security will not prevail; hence; the Judiciary must ensure speedy trials of suspects and promote the rule of law as well as check the arbitrary actions of the Legislature and Executive intended to undermine good governance.

Basically, the actions of the international community are intended to foster an agenda for peace, recovery, economic growth and national development. These interventions must be bolstered by political cohesion, and religious commitment to the separation of powers, amongst the three branches of government in the best interest of the state. All branches of government must deliver on their mandates to ensure that the citizens in post-war Liberia accrue maximum benefits from the intervention of foreign partners. While it is true that donors and international partners largely preside over resources intended for Liberia's recovery, the Government must maximize its own resources for the good of Liberia. This requires rigorous budgetary process and a compassionate resource allocation in the budget based on needs of local communities, as well as a thorough dealing with corrupt officials and practices.

6.3 Challenges Requiring Action:

The origin of Liberia's political, economic and social maladies is grounded on key issues. These key issues pose a major challenge to checks and balances to national government. For instance, significant portions of society were systematically excluded and marginalized from institutions of political governance and access to key economic assets. The founding constitution was designed for the needs of the settler population, with less consideration and involvement of the indigenous people. In the early days, land and property rights of most Liberians were severely limited. Later, marginalization was perpetuated by the urban-based policies of successive administrations.

Political power was concentrated in Monrovia and primarily at the Presidency. Most infrastructure and basic services were concentrated in Monrovia and a few other cities. Marginalization of youth and women, mismanagement of national resources, and inequalities in the distribution of benefits were significant problems. The over-concentration of power bred corruption, restricted access to the decision-making process, and limited the space for civil society participation in the process of governance. The consequence was a high level of resentment towards the ruling elite, which in part led to the bloody military coup of 1980 and its initial support among the people. Unfortunately, the military and successive governments later failed to correct the ills of society and expanded the problems.

Second, economic collapse helped fuel the crisis. Liberia's economy enjoyed steady economic growth averaging 4 to 7 percent per year through the 1960s, but most of the gains were heavily concentrated within the elite, and most Liberians saw little benefit. The economy began to dwindle in the 1970s with the combination of the sharp increase in world petroleum prices and the decline in the prices of key export commodities. By the latter part of the decade all indicators pointed to a looming crisis. Unemployment, consumer prices, and food prices all rose at alarming rates, growth stagnated, and tensions rose sharply.

The damage and negative consequences of the conflict were enormous. Commercial and productive activities ceased as various warlords looted and vandalized the country. Families were shattered; entire communities were uprooted. The entire social, political, economic, and traditional systems of governance were destroyed. There was massive exodus of skills and talents from the country. The economy completely collapsed. GDP fell from a catastrophic 90% between 1987 and 1995, one of the largest economic collapses ever recorded in the world (World Bank Development Indicators, 2007). By the time of the elections in 2005, average income in Liberia was just one-quarter of what it had been in 1987, and just one-sixth of its level in 1979.

Agricultural production dropped as people fled their farms and the supporting infrastructure collapsed; mining and timber activities were shut down, rubber plantations closed, manufacturing essentially stopped, and services grounded to a halt. Production of iron ore, timber, and mining ceased completely. Rice production fell below 73% between 1987 and 2005, financial services fell below 93%, and electricity and water fell below 85%. Transportation and communication, trade and hotels, and construction all fell around 70%; only the production of charcoal and wood increased as Liberians turned to these products to meet their basic energy needs (World Bank Development Indicators, 2007).

Basic infrastructure was destroyed. Many roads are impassable, which seriously constrains peace building efforts, economic activity, and the provision of basic health and education services. Unemployment soars, and poverty increases sharply, with more than 61 percent of Liberians now living below the poverty line. Schools, hospitals, and clinics are badly damaged, and most government buildings are in shambles. There are less than 50 Liberian Medical Doctors to cover the nation's public health needs, equal to one for every 70,000 Liberians. About 70 percent of school buildings were partially or wholly destroyed, and over half of Liberian children and youth are estimated to be out of school. A whole generation of Liberians has spent more time at war than in school. Public finances collapsed, with annual revenue falling to $85 million, allowing per capita public expenditure of about US$25, one of the lowest levels in the world. The past governments defaulted on their debts, and by 2006 external debt had increased to US$4.5 billion; though it has now been cleared due to the Government's completion of HIPC requirements, but it is gradually growing again due to budget deficits and the pressing need to borrow and invest in infrastructure reconstruction.

Domestic debt and arrears added an additional US$900 million, of which about US$300 million was ultimately deemed valid by external examiners. Despite considerable progress since the end of the civil war largely caused by the inadequacies of the three branches of government, Liberia still confronts formidable reconstruction and development challenges. The legacy of despotism, conflict and social disintegration - coupled with pervasive poverty, food insecurity, illiteracy and unemployment – constrain Liberia's efforts to promote recovery. To address this, all three branches of the Government of Liberia must revitalize public institutions and press forward with reforms. The direct and intensive engagement of the Liberian people in guiding policy choices and substantive transformation process is essential to the success of reconstruction and development.

The branches of government must welcome the Poverty Reduction Strategy (PRS) 2008-2011 but ensure full implementation of the CDAs because they evolved from a consultative process that took the views of counties and districts into account, thus making it a highly constructive means of consolidating the progress toward national development. The National Legislature must ensure, through prudent budgetary allocation, the right to food, healthcare, safe water and sanitation, shelter and education as fundamental human rights.

The state has begun to rebuild the full range of its security forces and made substantial progress in reintegrating refugees and IDPs, with strong support from its international partners. It demobilized and reintegrated over 90,000 ex-combatants through formal reintegration programs and deactivated or retired over 17,000 members of the Armed Forces of Liberia (AFL), the Liberian National Police, and the Special Security Service. At the same time, it has begun to recruit and train the "new AFL and police force". It has renovated the Police Academy Training Facilities and concluded plans for the construction of several county headquarters with police depots around the country.

The Government in early 2006 immediately cancelled all forestry contracts and reviewed 95 contracts and concessions granted by the Transitional Government, and subsequently passed a Forest Reform Act to strengthen oversight and regulation of the forestry sector. These steps paved the way for the United Nations Security Council to lift the sanctions on Liberian timber exports and should have led to a rapid recovery in the timber sector during the PRS period. The Government completed negotiations with Arcelor Mittal Steel (and the Firestone Rubber Company) to revise major concession agreements to increase the benefits for the Liberian people and concluded new agreements to re-start oil palm production. Although, the Firestone Agreement still hurts the state in terms of its benefits to the people; more must be done to ensure that all the new concession agreements signed bring more benefits to the people of Liberia. One fundamental question remains that: will Liberia continue to export raw materials? Exporting raw materials means an exportation of most needed jobs in Liberia. Can the Legislature ensure that all these concessions operating in Liberia begin to construct factories or manufacturing plants that will manufacture some finished and semi-finished products prior to shipment out of Liberia? This is the time to take corrective measures and build a unified, developed and prosperous country in which Liberians will be proud to remain and where foreigners will find reasons to settle? The time is now.

Liberia needs to revisit her investment policies and laws. Foreign investors or traders should not just be granted licenses to operate businesses and investments in Liberia. Investment must be based on national interest, where investors must partner with Liberians and make them managers of businesses. This partnership will ensure that the departure of investors or foreign businesses would not leave a vacuum as has been over the years. All businesses in Liberia must be done with Liberian partnerships. The oil companies need to partner with Liberian businessmen and women, so should be the mining companies, etc. Retail businesses should solely be left to Liberians. If ordinary Liberians do not have the assets to become investment partners, then the Government must become the bigger share holder in these concessions so that the state and concessionaires would share profits. Investors should not get richer on our resources, while the country and its people get poorer.

As these achievements and others show, Liberia has made substantial progress in the last few years. Many challenges lie ahead, but with strong support from its partners and the eager participation of the Liberian people, the Government could lay the foundation for rapid, sustained, and shared growth and development in the years to come. With the country at peace and the initial recovery now clearly underway, Liberia is well positioned to continue expanding economic opportunities, delivering basic services throughout the country, and re-building the institutions needed for equitable growth, wealth creation, and a transparent government. Accountable Government needs an accountable, effective and efficient Legislature and Judiciary. Can they stand up to the task? History will be the best judge.

CHAPTER VII

CONCLUSION AND WAY FORWARD

7. 1 Conclusion

So far, this research underscores the need for the balance of power in the Republic of Liberia. The Executive branch dominates power politics in Liberia because it does not only have abounding resources, but also controls regional administrations, manipulates the Judiciary and controls legislators who are weak and sometimes poorly educated and indigent. Poverty, greed, ignorance, and unpatriotic attitudes hinder legislators' independence in delivering on their mandates.

Unlike other western countries like the United States of America, where legislative powers are maximally exercised, the legislature in Liberia has been defaulting in checking and balancing power with the other two branches. In the wake of this, the executive overshadows the operation of government. Sometimes, the president expends government resources, enters concession agreements with foreign investors, ignoring the legislators' acquiescence. Since the Republic of Liberia has three distinct, but coordinate branches of government whose functions are deeply rooted in the constitution, the legislators, among other things, have to approve national budgets and authorize national expenditures on presidential travels; sanction security and defense matters; evolve an environment for international partnership; create palatable conditions for citizenship; residence, etc. It is obvious that without the Legislative branch, the government cannot secure its territorial integrity, provide the basic social services for its people, and interact with regional and international bodies for trade and diplomacy. In short, the Legislature is the point of commencement for the protection of Liberia's national interest.

Henceforth, it is expected that the Legislators will save the country by enacting transformative laws in the interest of the majority. It must be checked by both the Judiciary and Executive such that ruthless and ambiguous laws are not enacted against the national interest of the state. The desired Legislature that this research tends to proffer as an alternative to past and current ones is an efficient and effective Legislature devoid of greed, selfishness, corruption, ineptitude and didactic political maneuvering. The balance of power can be achieved when the Executive disengages from the undue usurpation of the powers of the other branches or is checked by the other two branches (Judiciary and Legislature). Howbeit, this requires legislative and judicial alertness to check arbitrary and deliberate executive actions meant to undermine checks and balances. There could be balance of power when the Legislature is politically conscious of its duties and responsibilities, checks the actions of the Executive and Judiciary, and puts the interests of citizens first. The representative democracy to which Liberia subscribes also calls for respect for public opinion, without which it becomes difficult to measure the performance of a democratic system anywhere in the world.

As this research is intended to reawaken the Liberian National Legislature to assume its rightful place, help curb presidential misuse and abuse of power, encourage judicial independence and trigger formulation of public policies and laws in the general interest of the people, it is my ardent hope that current and future lawmakers would find it useful to spare sometime and read through these pages, even if they disagree. Our agreements and disagreement would only help to make the

Liberian democracy stronger than weaker. In short, it tends to advocate for checks and balances amongst the three branches of government as enshrined in the Constitution. Thus far, I have showcased selected historical highlights on Presidential dominance in the country, the weakness of the Legislature and the lukewarm conduct of the Judiciary. I have investigated the operationalization of the principle of checks and balances as enshrined in the Liberian constitution, provided insights on some of the lapses and made pragmatic suggestions that our national government could consider making further advances in transforming our motherland.

It is hoped that this piece of research, which, in many ways, is neither exhaustive nor a panacea to the numerous challenges, will help to bring a crude awakening to citizens, political parties, religious groups and civil society to eschew political apathy and participate in the debate on socio-political and economic transformation of our dear country. I also hope this piece of research will provoke a scholarly debate, whereby Liberian and foreign scholars can step up to the plate and suggest alternative options that can engender an effective legislature in the framework of the republican form of government that Liberia subscribes to.

Indeed, the powers of the Legislature are agreeably broad. They go beyond enacting laws. Its powers encompass the supervision and conduct of oversight over the Judiciary and the Executive in their respective interpretation and enforcement of the law. The First Branch can invite any member of the Cabinet, Judiciary and hold them in contempt. Yet, with all these powers, the legislators are practically dependent on the Executive. The reason is that many Liberian legislators are poor, ignorant, inexperienced and virtually illiterate; hence, they fight to entrench themselves in the elite class by compromising the interests of their constituents. They tend to forget that progressive, transformative and pro-poor laws will alleviate poverty, ignorance, inexperience, illiteracy and corruption.

To conclude, as this writing progresses, presidential autocracy persists in Liberia at the disadvantage of the people with whom power rests. To redeem the state from an Executive autocracy, the Legislature should become effective in exercising her constitutional roles, ranging from making good laws to providing security and common defense for the state; declaring war and authorizing the Executive to conclude peace; levying taxes on high income earners, not imposed on the impoverished, but intended to increased national revenues paid high income earners and investors; establishing inferior courts to the Supreme Court; confirming presidential nominees, not on the basis of bribes, but on the basis of qualification and meritocracy; approving treaties; impeaching the President and other government officials for proven misconduct, and raising the national army, among others (the Constitution 2000). These roles may forever be cosmetic, if neglected, downplayed and forgotten by the Liberian Legislature.

7.2 Way Forward

According to Article 34 of the 1986 Constitution of Liberia, the Legislature has the power to create new counties, provide for the security and defense of the Republic, declare war and mandate the Executive to conclude peace, raise the national army, impose or levy taxes, issue currency, borrow loans, create subordinate courts, approve treaties or conventions, regulate trade and commerce, make laws for citizenship, residence, and naturalization, make election laws, and enact laws for pension scheme. The powers of the Legislature are arguably broad, yet they have not been effectively used. In the face of these huge responsibilities, history has shown that many a time lawmaker were illiterate, incompetent, corrupt and greedy, thereby making them weak, ineffective and inefficient. To solve this problem, those to be elected should be well educated, sound and or competent, they should have integrity and progressive track record in society and be reform oriented, and well informed about the law-making process. At least a minimum of college graduate or above should serve as legislators. They should likewise be knowledgeable about issues needing changes based on national interest, as well as capable to performing all other duties assigned them.

Additionally, it can be recalled that the Legislature has been induced by the patronage system of the Executive as earlier discussed. In this light, it would be expedient if those to be voted for as legislative candidates can possess modest properties and honest substantive financial or economic stature. If this happens, lawmakers could stop being subservient to the patronage scheme of the Executive, though this does not necessarily mean that non-property owners of age 25 and 30 should not contest as lawmakers as there is sometimes the tendency of those having more wanting even more; hence, the issues of integrity and honesty, as well as love for the country being the ultimate values on which legislators should be elected.

Furthermore, the Legislature, which has the constitutional mandate to authorize government expenditures, must ensure that government funds are appropriately allocated for the benefit of constituencies or counties rather than giving the Executive upper hand in deciding who gets what and which projects get supported by the people's taxes. The proposed budget of any President can be rejected and recast before legislative endorsement. National budget allocation should place emphasis on agriculture, infrastructural development, health, education as advancement in these sectors would help reduce dependence on civil service positions. There should be government-sponsored scholarships to bolster education in all sectors. Particularly, the National Legislature should introduce the "Liberian styled Higher Education Contribution Scheme" under which impoverished university students could get financial support from government and repay upon completion of their degrees and commencement of job.

In a related manner, the Executive needs to be accountable to the Legislature, not just delivering an annual report as a formality and declaring rerun for presidency. Similarly, the Senate must ensure that those nominated by the President for its approval be qualified to serve in their designated capacities. Many times, confirmation hearings do not critically examine past political, economic, ethical and social records. This must be improved on.

More so, the lawmakers should seek recourse to their constituencies in times of policy decisions that will affect those constituencies. The Legislature should demand that the Executive conclude peace in times of crisis to save the people from future conflicts and civil unrests. The Legislature must exercise impeachment proceedings in times of misrule by the Executive or Judiciary rather than being sympathetic to the ruling party's interest. It is evident that impeachment proceedings in the past helped to checkmate and deter elected Presidents from contravening the organic laws of the land. The Legislature must propagate all constitutional obligations without fear or favor so that the essence of a Republican government can be realized.

The citizens, for their part, need to elect legislators that will specifically guarantee their interests. Without the people and civil society as watchdogs, the Legislature will pursue selfish motives; hence; the need for citizens and civil society to hold government officials accountable. In this venture, the people have a responsibility, and the Legislature is obliged to protect the interest of their people. According to Cllr. Wagner (2000) "the Liberian citizens created the 1986 constitution and the responsibility rests solely with them to ensure that it lives on in posterity. It shall exist only by their resolve. Losing their resolve or neglecting to keep vigilant watch on anyone who would seek to rule outside its provisions will ensure its destruction."

Having discovered from this research that accountability is decreasing in government since the twentieth century governments under which executive usurpation of the legislature duties germinated, and that some legislators do not have sound, proper and or professional educational upbringings;

Cognizant of the fact that the constitution allows for the election of some local officials like Chiefs, but gives the President power to remove them;

Knowing that the President enjoys enormous powers over county authorities, and that he or she has the constitutional right to nominate legal-minded persons for their approval by the senate and onward employment in the Judiciary;

Aware that the Vice President casts a vote in the event of a tie in the Senate vote, an act that could compromise the integrity of the Senate since the Vice President is subservient to the President;

Conscious of the fact that there exists no laws prohibiting presidents from appointing legislators to other positions of trust, thereby sometimes making them vacate the Senate or the House of Representatives through appointments to "lucrative" positions; and aware of the fact that the legislators must make laws to raise the National Army, authorize war or conclude peace, levy taxes, provide for the security and defense of the country, etc.,

It is hereby further recommended that:

Legislators are at least college or university graduates with prior working experience in local, national government or international circles.

The Legal Bar Association of Liberia should elect a team of lawyers from whence the Chief Executive should nominate the Chief Justice, Associate Justices, and Judges for the Senate's confirmation, and subsequent employment in the Judiciary. This might increase independence of the Judiciary.

There should be constitutional amendment to nullify the election of traditional chiefs whose election undermines Liberia's traditional heritage and values.

The Vice President is barred from casting a vote in the event of a tie in the Senate because this could compromise the integrity of the Senate since the Vice President is subservient to the President. It also brings about an imbalance in the representation of counties in that the Vice President might cast a vote in favor or his/her county against the interest of other counties.

The operations of the military are sanctioned by the Legislative Branch.

County superintendents are elected in order to make them accountable to their people rather than the President.

Fines and levies charged by the courts be deposited in designated government bank accounts to avoid misappropriation by judicial workers;

Legislative tenure is reduced from six to four years for Representatives and from nine to five years for Senators, both with a limit of two terms.

The tenure of President is reduced from six to four years, with a limit of two terms only.

The Senate ratifies removal of government officials previously confirmed by the Senate for Presidential appointment. This will contain the arbitrary removal of appointed officials.

There should be a constitutional amendment prohibiting any legislator from migrating from the party on which he/she was elected to another while serving a term, or if a legislator wishes to change party, then a re-election should be called for replacement.

The Government of the Republic of Liberia uphold the principles of the Constitution of the Republic of Liberia, most especially paying keen attention to **CHAPTER I: GENERAL PRINCIPLES OF NATIONAL POLICY, which states the following:**

"**Article 4:** The principles contained in this Chapter shall be fundamental in the governance of the Republic and shall serve as guidelines in the formulation of legislative, executive and administrative directives, policy-making and their execution.

Article 5: The Republic shall:

a) aim at strengthening the national integration and unity of the people of Liberia, regardless of ethnic, regional or other differences, into one body politic; and the Legislature shall enact laws promoting national unification and the encouragement of all citizens to participate in government;

b) preserve, protect and promote positive Liberian culture, ensuring that traditional values which are compatible with public policy and national progress are adopted and developed as an integral part of the growing needs of the Liberian society;

c) take steps, by appropriate legislation and executive orders, to eliminate sectionalism and tribalism, and such abuses of power as the misuse of government resources, nepotism and all other corrupt practices.

Article 6: The Republic shall, because of the vital role assigned to the individual citizen under this Constitution for the social, economic and political well being of Liberia, provide equal access to educational opportunities and facilities for all citizens to the extent of available resources. Emphasis shall be placed on the mass education of the Liberian people and the elimination of illiteracy.

Article 7: The Republic shall, consistent with the principles of individual freedom and social justice enshrined in this Constitution, manage the national economy and the natural resources of Liberia in such manner as shall ensure the maximum feasible participation of Liberian citizens under conditions of equality as to advance the general welfare of the Liberian people and the economic development of Liberia.

Article 8: The Republic shall direct its policy towards ensuring for all citizens, without discrimination, opportunities for employment and livelihood under just and humane conditions, and towards promoting safety, health and welfare facilities in employment.

Article 9: The Republic shall encourage the promotion of bilateral and regional cooperation between and among Liberia and other nations and the formation and maintenance of regional organizations aimed at the cultural, social, political and economic development of the peoples of Africa and other nations of the world.

Article 10: The Republic shall ensure the publication and dissemination of this Constitution throughout the Republic and the teaching of its principles and provisions in all institutions of learning in Liberia".

Bibliography

Africa Infrastructure Country Diagnostic Report 2010, Liberia Infrastructure, A continental Perspective, viewed 7 March 2014, <http://siteresources.worldbank.org/INTAFRICA/Resources/Liberia-Country_Report_03.2011.pdf>.

Agenda for Transformation (AfT) 2013, Ministry of Finance, Government of Liberia, viewed 7 March 2014, < mof.gov.lr/doc/AfT%20document-%20April%2015, %202013.pdf>.

Annual Report 2007, National Commission on Disarmament, Demobilization, Rehabilitation and Reintegration (NCDDRR).

Boley, S 1983, *Liberia, the Rise and Fall of the First Republic*, Macmillan, London and Basingstoke.

Clower R, 1966, *Growth Without Development: An Economic Survey of Liberia*, Clower Northwestern University Press.

Economic and Social Commission for Asian and the Pacific review report (nd.), *Eco-efficient and sustainable urban infrastructure development in Asia and Latin America*, Viewed on 7 March 2014, <http://www.unescap.org/esd/environment/infra/suncheon/background-studies.asp>.

Elwood, D, Beyan, A & Burrowes, C 2001, *Historical Dictionary of Liberia*, 2nd ed., Scarecrow Press.

Guanu, J 2005, *Liberian History and Government an Overview Pamphlet*, Cuttington University.

_____ 2000, *A Short History of the First Liberian Republic, Sequel to Liberian History up to 1847*, 2nd edition.

Hlopher, S 1979, *Class, Ethnicity and Politics in Liberia: A Class Analysis of Power Struggles in the Tubman and Tolbert Administration from 1944-1975*, University Press of America, 1979.

Huberich, C 1947, *The Political and Legislature History of Liberia, Volume I,* Central Book Company, Inc. New York.

Kaydor, T 2002, An *Effective Legislature: An Alternative to Presidential Autocracy in Liberia,* Undergraduate Thesis (unpublished), University of Liberia, Monrovia.

Legislative Report Card 2007, Catholic Justice and Peace Commission, Monrovia, Liberia.

International Monetary Fund 2012, IMF Country Report No. 12/45 viewed 30 March 2014, < www.imf.org/external/pubs/ft/scr/2012/cr1245.pdf>.

Liberia Institute of Statistics and Geo-Information Services (LISGIS) 2007, *Liberia Demographic and Health Survey (2007)*, Liberia Institute of Statistics and Geo-Information Services (LISGIS), Monrovia, Liberia.

Liberian Legislature Strategic Development Plan 2008-2012, National Legislature, Capitol Hill, Monrovia, Liberia.

Liberia Institute of Statistics and Geo-Information Services (LISGIS) 2008, *National Census Report*, Government of Liberia, Monrovia, Liberia.

Liberian Journal of Democracy 1999, Vol. 1, NO. 1, Monrovia, Liberia.

Liberia Poverty Reduction Strategy 2007, Ministry of Planning and Economic Affairs, Government of Liberia.

'Liberia Rising Vision 2030' 2013, Ministry of Finance, Government of Liberia, viewed 7 March 2014 < mof.gov.lr/doc/AfT%20document-%20April%2015,%202013.pdf>.

Liebenow, G 1987, *Liberia, the Quest for Democracy*, Indiana University Press, Bloomington and Indianapolis.

_____ 1969, *Liberia, the Evolution of privilege*, Cornell University Press, Ithaca and London.

Making Democracy Work in Liberia: The Constitution 2000, University of Liberia Press.

Melusky, J 2000, *The American Political System; An Owner's Manual*, 1st edition, McGraw-Hill Companies

Ministry of Education 2009, *Education Sector Policy*, Government of Liberia, viewed 31 March 2014, <planipolis.iiep.unesco.org/upload/Liberia/Liberia_Sector_Plan.pdf>.

Ministry of Planning and Economic Affairs 2013, Government of Liberia, Republic of Liberia Agenda for Transformation: Steps Towards Liberia Rising 2030, viewed 11 March 2014

< mof.gov.lr/doc/AfT%20document-%20April%2015,%202013.pdf>.

Monash University Library (nd.), *How to Write the Case Study*, QuickRef27, viewed 21 March 2014, <www.monash.edu.au/lls/llonline/quickrefs/27-case-study.pdf>.

Moteff J and Parfomak P 2004, *Critical Infrastructure and Key Assets: Definition and Identification, Congressional Research*

Services, the Library of Congress, viewed 7 March 2014, < https://www.fas.org/sgp/crs/RL32631.pdf>.

Results Focused Transition Framework (RFTF) 2005, Ministry of Planning and Economic Affairs, Government of Liberia.

Rosenstein-Rodan 1957, *Notes on the Theory of the 'big Push'*, Center for International Studies, Massachusetts Institute of Technology, USA.

Sawyer, A 1992, *The Emergence of Autocracy in Liberia: Tragedy and Challenge*, ICS, San Francisco, California.

The Comprehensive Peace Agreement 2003, Accra, Ghana.

The Liberia Poverty Reduction Strategy (PRS) 2008, Ministry of Planning and Economic Affairs, Republic of Liberia.

The World Bank 2010, *Liberia GPD per capital estimate cited in United Nations in Liberia 2013, One programme: The UN Development Assistance Framework (UNDAF 2013-2017)*, Monrovia, viewed 14 January 2014, <http://unliberia.org/doc/undaf_doc.pdf>.

Project Liberia 2014, viewed 21 March 2014, <http://www.wavesforwater.org/project/Project-Liberia>.

The World Bank 2007, *World Bank World Development Indicator.*

Travers, R 2005, *Patriotic Leadership, The pathway to Democracy and Opportunity*, ed. Anchrey Bell- Keorney, TPG, Blackwood, NJ.

United Nations Liberia, *The United Nations Development Assistance Framework (UNDAF)* 2008, Revised.

United Nations in Liberia 2013, One programme: The UN Development Assistance Framework (UNDAF 2013-2017), Monrovia, viewed 14 January 2014, <http://unliberia.org/doc/undaf_doc.pdf>.

United Nations Development Programme 2013, *Human Development Index*, New York, viewed 20 March 2014, <http://www.undp.org/content/undp/en/home/presscenter/pressreleases/2013/03/14/human-development-index-in-2013-report-shows-major-gains-since-2000-in-most-countries-of-south/>.

World Commission on Environment and Development (WCED) (1987), *Our common Future,* Oxford: Oxford University Press, viewed 10 March 2014,

< conspect.nl/pdf/Our_Common_Future-Brundtland_Report_1987.pdf>.

Wreh, T 1976, The Love of Liberty ... The Rule of President William V.S. Tubman in Liberia 1944-1971, C Hurst and Company, London.

Youboty, J 2004, *A Nation in Terror, The True story of the Liberian Civil War*, USA.

Newspaper, blogs, links & others
The New Democrat newspaper, Monrovia, Liberia.
The New Dawn Newspaper, Monrovia, Liberia.
Public Agenda Newspaper, Monrovia, Liberia.
Daily Observer Newspaper, Monrovia, Liberia.
UN Panel of Experts Report on Liberia 2003.
UN Panel of Experts Report on Liberia 2006.
UN Panel of Experts Report on Liberia 2007.
The Newark Advocate, April 22, 1984; viewed 23 January 2014
http://personal.denison.edu/~waite/liberia/history/roye.htm.

Thomas Kaydor, Jr.

http://en.wikipedia.org/wiki/President_of_Liberia.

http://memory.loc.gov/ammem/gmdhtml/libhtml/liberia.html.

http://onliberia.org/con_index.htm.

http://frontpageafricaonline.blogspot.com.au/2011/04/justice-for-sale.html.

http://tomkaydor.blogspot.com.au/, viewed 19 March 2014.

http://makingdemocracymatter.blogspot.com/, viewed 19 March 2014.

ANNEX I: LIST OF PRESIDENTS OF LIBERIA

None   Republican Party   True Whig Party   National Democratic Party   National Patriotic Party   Unity Party

#	President		Took office	Left office	Party	Vice President(s)
1	Joseph Jenkins Roberts		January 3, 1848	January 7, 1856	none (Republican policies)	Stephen Allen Benson
2	Stephen Allen Benson		January 7, 1856	January 4, 1864	none (Republican policies)	Beverley Yates
3	Daniel Bashiel Warner		January 4, 1864	January 6, 1868	Republican Party	James M. Priest
4	James Spriggs Payne		January 6, 1868	January 3, 1870	Republican Party	*Vacant*
5	Edward James Roye		January 3, 1870	October 26, 1871[A]	True Whig Party	James Skivring Smith
6	James Skivring Smith[4]		November 4, 1871	January 1, 1872	True Whig Party	Anthony W. Gardiner
7	Joseph Jenkins Roberts (*2nd term*)		January 1, 1872	January 3, 1876	Republican Party	Anthony W. Gardiner

8	James Spriggs Payne *(2nd term)*		January 3, 1876	January 7, 1878	Republican Party	*Vacant*
9	Anthony W. Gardiner		January 7, 1878	January 20, 1883[R]	True Whig Party	Alfred Francis Russell
10	Alfred Francis Russell		January 20, 1883	January 7, 1884	True Whig Party	*Vacant*
11	Hilary R. W. Johnson		January 7, 1884	January 4, 1892	True Whig Party	*Vacant*
12	Joseph James Cheeseman		January 4, 1892	November 12, 1896[D]	True Whig Party	William D. Coleman
13	William D. Coleman		November 12, 1896	December 11, 1900[R]	True Whig Party	J. J. Ross
14	Garreston W. Gibson		December 11, 1900	January 4, 1904	True Whig Party	*Vacant*
15	Arthur Barclay		January 4, 1904	January 1, 1912	True Whig Party	J. J. Dossen
16	Daniel Edward Howard		January 1, 1912	January 5, 1920	True Whig Party	*Vacant*

17	Charles D. B. King		January 5, 1920	December 3, 1930[R]	True Whig Party	Samuel Alfred Ross Henry Too Wesley Allen Yancy
18	Edwin Barclay		December 3, 1930	January 3, 1944	True Whig Party	*Vacant*
19	William Tubman		January 3, 1944	July 23, 1971[D]	True Whig Party	Clarence Lorenzo Simpson William R. Tolbert, Jr.
20	William R. Tolbert, Jr.		July 23, 1971	April 12, 1980[A]	True Whig Party	James Edward Greene Bennie Dee Warner
21	Samuel Doe[S]		January 6, 1986	September 9, 1990[A]	National Democratic Party of Liberia	Harry Moniba
22	Charles Taylor		August 2, 1997	August 11, 2003[R]	National Patriotic Party	Enoch Dogolea Moses Blah
23	Moses Blah		August 11, 2003	October 14, 2003[R]	National Patriotic Party	*Vacant*
24	Ellen Johnson Sirleaf		January 16, 2006	Incumbent	Unity Party	Joseph Boakai

- **Left office early: [A] Assassinated in a *coup d'etat;* [D] Died in office of natural causes; [R] Resigned.**

ANNEX II: INTERIM AND NON-PRESIDENTIAL HEADS OF STATE

None National Democratic Party Liberian People's Party Liberian Action Party

President		Position	Took office	Left office	Party
Samuel K. Doe		Head of People's Redemption Council	April 12, 1980	January 6, 1986	National Democratic Party of Liberia
Dr. Amos Sawyer		President of the Interim Government of National Unity	November 22, 1990	March 7, 1994	Liberian People's Party
David D. Kpormakpor		Chairman of the Council of State	March 7, 1994	September 1, 1995	None
Wilton G. S. Sankawulo		Chairman of the Council of State	September 1, 1995	September 3, 1996	None
Ruth Perry		Chairwoman of the Council of State	September 3, 1996	August 2, 1997	None
Gyude Bryant		Chairman of the National Transitional Government	October 14, 2003	January 16, 2006	Liberian Action Party

ANNEX II: ADMINISTRATIVE MAP OF
LIBERIA BY POPULATION 2008

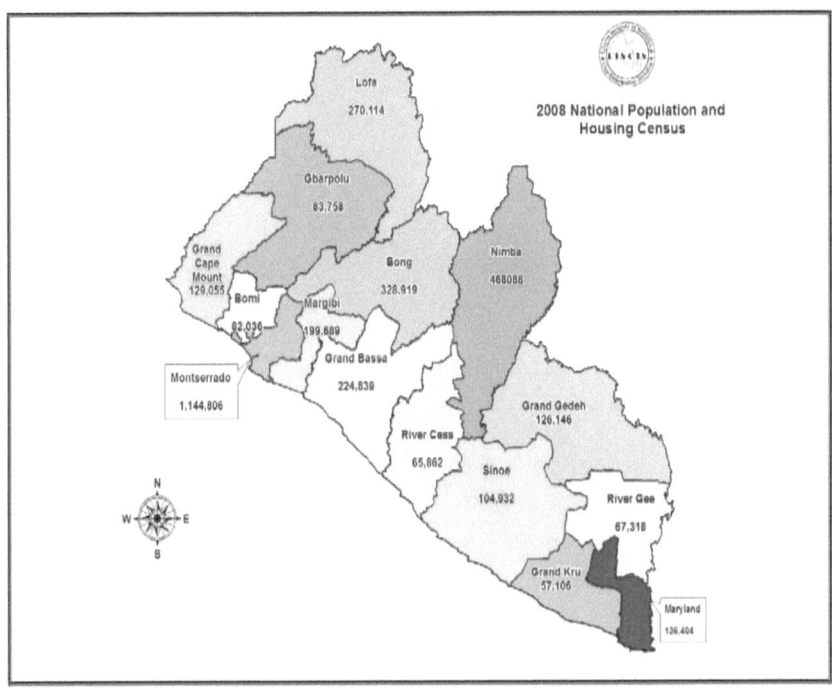

Figure 1.1 Liberia Administrative Map by Population 2008
(LISGIS CENSUS REPORT)

www.ingramcontent.com/pod-product-compliance
Lightning Source LLC
Chambersburg PA
CBHW020540290526
45786CB00002B/965